Learning Disabilities

Meryl Loonin

LUCENT BOOKS

A part of Gale, Cengage Learning

GALE
CENGAGE Learning·

Detroit • New York • San Francisco • New Haven, Conn • Waterville, Maine • London

LIBRARY OF CONGRESS CATALOGING-IN-PUBLICATION DATA

Loonin, Meryl.
   Learning disabilities / by Meryl Loonin.
      p. cm. -- (Diseases and disorders)
   Summary: "This series objectively and thoughtfully explores topics of medical importance. Books include sections on a description of the disease or disorder and how it affects the body, as well as diagnosis and treatment of the condition"-- Provided by publisher.
   Includes bibliographical references and index.
   ISBN 978-1-4205-0793-5 (hardback)
   1. Learning disabled. 2. Learning disabled--Treatment. I. Title.
   RC394.L37L66 2012
   616.85'889--dc23
                                                            2012002753=

Lucent Books
27500 Drake Rd.
Farmington Hills, MI 48331

ISBN-13: 978-1-4205-0793-5
ISBN-10: 1-4205-0793-1

Printed in the United States of America
1 2 3 4 5 6 7 16 15 14 13 12

Table of Contents

"The Most Difficult Puzzles Ever Devised"

Charles Best, one of the pioneers in the search for a cure for diabetes, once explained what it is about medical research that intrigued him so. "It's not just the gratification of knowing one is helping people," he confided, "although that probably is a more heroic and selfless motivation. Those feelings may enter in, but truly, what I find best is the feeling of going toe to toe with nature, of trying to solve the most difficult puzzles ever devised. The answers are there somewhere, those keys that will solve the puzzle and make the patient well. But how will those keys be found?"

Since the dawn of civilization, nothing has so puzzled people—and often frightened them, as well—as the onset of illness in a body or mind that had seemed healthy before. A seizure, the inability of a heart to pump, the sudden deterioration of muscle tone in a small child—being unable to reverse such conditions or even to understand why they occur was unspeakably frustrating to healers. Even before there were names for such conditions, even before they were understood at all, each was a reminder of how complex the human body was, and how vulnerable.

While our grappling with understanding diseases has been frustrating at times, it has also provided some of humankind's most heroic accomplishments. Alexander Fleming's accidental discovery in 1928 of a mold that could be turned into penicillin has resulted in the saving of untold millions of lives. The isolation of the enzyme insulin has reversed what was once a death sentence for anyone with diabetes. There have been great strides in combating conditions for which there is not yet a cure, too. Medicines can help AIDS patients live longer, diagnostic tools such as mammography and ultrasounds can help doctors find tumors while they are treatable, and laser surgery techniques have made the most intricate, minute operations routine.

This "toe-to-toe" competition with diseases and disorders is even more remarkable when seen in a historical continuum. An astonishing amount of progress has been made in a very short time. Just two hundred years ago, the existence of germs as a cause of some diseases was unknown. In fact, it was less than 150 years ago that a British surgeon named Joseph Lister had difficulty persuading his fellow doctors that washing their hands before delivering a baby might increase the chances of a healthy delivery (especially if they had just attended to a diseased patient)!

Each book in Lucent's Diseases and Disorders series explores a disease or disorder and the knowledge that has been accumulated (or discarded) by doctors through the years. Each book also examines the tools used for pinpointing a diagnosis, as well as the various means that are used to treat or cure a disease. Finally, new ideas are presented—techniques or medicines that may be on the horizon.

Frustration and disappointment are still part of medicine, for not every disease or condition can be cured or prevented. But the limitations of knowledge are being pushed outward constantly; the "most difficult puzzles ever devised" are finding challengers every day.

Learning Differently

In 1937 Harry Sylvester walked into the small, three-story schoolhouse in his hometown in rural Maine for the first time. Sylvester loved being outdoors and working in the fields of his family farm. He could drive and operate a tractor by the age of ten and was skilled at repairing farm machinery. At school, however, he felt stupid. As hard as he tried, he could not recognize the letters in his first grade reader or match the pictures to the words on the page. Sylvester recalls:

> It all seemed like pretty simple tasks, but for me, it just simply didn't work. I think my teacher saw me as being bright enough, and if I would only pay attention I'd be able to do the work like the other students. Her first strategy was that if I stayed in at recess long enough, I would give in and do the workbook. The truth of the matter was, I would have done the workbook the very first day, if I could have. I stayed in for week after week—I don't really remember how long—and listened to the other kids playing at recess and having a wonderful time. I took my pencil and went back and forth on my reading workbook, and eventually I cut a slot right through the darned thing.[1]

Sylvester eventually became president of the Learning Disabilities Association of America. The story he relates in his memoir of being mistreated, humiliated, and bullied in school is the story of tens of thousands of learning-disabled children of his era who had trouble learning to read, write, solve math problems, and perform other academic tasks. They were punished in front of their peers or isolated in classrooms with other troubled children. Teachers believed that they were either mentally retarded (below average in intelligence as measured by a standardized IQ test) or lazy and unmotivated.

Today educators understand that there are children with learning disabilities whose brains take in information and process it differently than the brains of most other people. Although they are intelligent, they struggle with one or more aspects of speaking, listening, reading, writing, solving math problems, coordinating muscle movements, or interacting socially. When a child with a learning disability tries to accomplish an academic task, information gets stuck or slowed down while traveling through the brain.

Widespread and Unpredictable

Educators are more aware of children with learning disabilities than ever before, because they encounter them in their classrooms each year. More than 5 percent of U.S. students are identified with a learning disability and receive special education services in school. Yet the number of people with learning disabilities is probably much higher. Many people struggle in school, work, or everyday life, but their learning disabilities remain undetected. The National Center for Learning Disabilities (NCLD) estimates that between 10 and 15 percent of the U.S. population, or roughly one in every seven people, is learning disabled.

Learning disabilities are widespread, but they are also unpredictable. Their impact can range from mild to severe. Some people with these disabilities succeed in school and in the workplace. They become artists, doctors, lawyers, actors, writers, athletes, scientists, and political leaders. While there is no way to know for certain, U.S. president Woodrow Wilson may have been learning disabled. So, it is believed, was the brilliant inventor Thomas Edison and Nobel Prize–winning scientist Albert Einstein, both of whom had a remarkable ability to think in pictures but performed poorly in school. Yet too many children with learning disabilities struggle and never reach their potential. For every success story, there is another story of a learning-disabled child who grows frustrated and feels like a failure. More than 40 percent of students identified as learning disabled in America never earn a regular high school diploma. As adults, a disproportionate number live in poverty, suffer from depression, and remain unemployed for long stretches of time.

Toward a Greater Understanding

A child who is identified as learning disabled today has a much greater chance of succeeding in school and in life than at any time in the past. With advances in technology, researchers have begun to understand more about how learning takes place in the brain. Educators have developed effective strategies and interventions to support learning-disabled students. Federal laws protect them from discrimination and ensure that they are included in the regular education classroom. New

New assistive technologies, like the pictured voice recognition and text-to-speech software, make it easier for learning-disabled students to achieve their goals.

assistive technologies, such as voice recognition and text-to-speech software, also make it easier to help learning-disabled students achieve their goals. Despite such gains, schools are often harsh places for students who learn differently. Even today, many young people with learning disabilities report feeling frustrated, insecure, and angry in school.

Although this book is part of a series called Diseases and Disorders, a learning disability is not a disease. It cannot be cured or treated with medicine. A learning disability is often classified as a disorder, but some people reject that label because it implies that learning-disabled people are broken and in need of repair. Researchers often caution against defining people in terms of their disabilities. Instead, they say that learning-disabled people should be considered as individuals who have challenges and learn differently than others but who are not less smart nor incapable of learning. If they have the support of families, friends, teachers, and the larger community, and the self-understanding to know how they learn best, they can and do succeed.

CHAPTER ONE

What Is a Learning Disability?

I've been called many things throughout my life . . . *lazy, stupid, doesn't even try.* . . . My third grade math teacher doesn't believe me when I tell her I can't read the directions she has written on the board. Again and again I ask her to read them to me. She refuses. So I sit in my third grade math class and draw (the one thing I can do.) The teacher catches me and throws me out of class, saying I'm lazy, not even trying to do my work. I cry because I *want* to do well, to understand . . . to read. But I just can't, and I don't know why.[2]

In this passage, a young woman named Liana describes what it is like to grow up with a learning disability. People with learning disabilities often say they are confused, unsure of themselves, frustrated, or alone. They are intelligent, but they sometimes feel stupid because they have to work harder than other people to accomplish the same tasks. On the outside, they look like everyone else, but on the inside they feel different.

The term *learning disability* refers to a range of conditions in the brain that make it difficult for people to learn. It is hard to pin down an exact definition, because a learning disability can affect many skills, including reading, writing, speaking, listening, reasoning, solving math problems, coordinating muscle movements, or interacting socially. People who are learning disabled process information differently than other people. They are not sick and do not have a condition that can be treated with medicine. Yet there is something different in the way their brains are "wired," or connected, that interferes with the learning process. Trying to read a textbook, write a report, or solve a math problem with a learning disability is sometimes compared to driving down a highway that is backed up with slow-moving traffic due to road construction. When a person with a learning disability tries to accomplish an academic task, information gets slowed down or stuck while traveling through certain parts of the brain.

There is another reason that the term *learning disability* is hard to define, and that is that no two people with learning disabilities present in the same way. Each has a unique pattern of strengths and weaknesses. Some people struggle with a single area of learning; others have difficulty with several different areas. Some might have problems with learning to read and spell or with the ability to add and subtract, tell time, or follow directions. Others might grow frustrated trying to express their ideas in writing or to memorize new vocabulary. The impact of their disabilities on learning and everyday life can also vary from mild to severe.

While everyone with a learning disability is unique, there are certain characteristics they have in common. They are intelligent and have the capacity to learn. To be identified as learning disabled, a person must perform at the near average, average, or above average range on a standardized test of intelligence expressed as his or her IQ score. Yet because of their disabilities, there is a gap between what they are capable of achieving and what they actually achieve in school and at work that can be frustrating to them and the people around them. Another thing they have in common is that their disabilities are lifelong. They may develop strategies to compensate for areas of weakness, but their disabilities will not be cured or disappear, even as they grow older.

The Steps of the Learning Process

When a person has a learning disability, there is a breakdown somewhere in the learning process as information travels through the brain. Researchers sometimes describe the brain as if it were a sophisticated computer system. In such a model, there are four steps that must happen for learning to occur. These include (1) input, (2) integration (also called "processing"), (3) memory, and (4) output. Dr. Larry Silver, a psychiatrist who studies and writes about children with learning disabilities, describes the steps of the learning process this way: "The first step is input, getting information into the brain, primarily from the eyes and the ears. Once this information has arrived, the brain needs to make sense out of it, a process called integration. Next, the information must be stored and later retrieved, the memory process. Finally, the brain must send some kind of message back to the nerves and muscles—its output."[3]

In reality, learning does not take place in an orderly, sequential way. The brain is far more complex than a computer. It is always active and finding new meaning in the information that arrives from the eyes, ears, and other senses. Yet this simplified model helps to explain how even a small disturbance at one step can have an impact on the entire system.

In the first step of the learning process, input, the brain takes in sensory information from the eyes, ears, and other senses. A person with a disability that disrupts the input step may see and hear perfectly well. The problem is in perception, how the brain receives the information that arrives at its visual or auditory pathways. A perception problem can interfere with learning to read, write, solve math equations, or coordinate movements. If the breakdown is in visual perception, a person might confuse the position and shape of letters and numbers or struggle to distinguish an object in the foreground of a picture from those in the background. She might also misjudge distances and constantly bump into things. If the problem interferes with auditory input, she might have trouble distinguishing similar sounds, or hearing what a teacher or classmate is saying over the background noise from the other students in the class.

In the second step, integration, or processing, the brain makes sense of new information and compares it with information that it has already received. There are many aspects of integration and many different ways in which a disruption at this step can interfere with learning. A person might struggle with

A learning-disabled person may have an issue with the input step of the learning process and perception. This can interfere with learning to read, write, solve math equations, or coordinate movements.

The Gift of a Learning Disability

When children are young and struggling under the intense pressures of the school environment, it is hard to conceive of a learning disability as a "gift." Yet many successful learning-disabled adults say the key to overcoming their weaknesses lay in discovering areas of unique strength or talent. Jamie Janover is a professional musician and photographer who had a hard time learning to read and write. He was always falling behind in his school assignments. Yet even as a young child, he had a "profound reaction" to music and art:

> I was totally fascinated with music, especially. When I was really young, my parents would put on music with a strong beat and I would go crazy by dancing all around. I also would bang on pots and pans. By the time, I was 14 I had saved enough money to get a drum kit. . . . As a kid, my brain had pockets of amazing creativity, energy, insightfulness, and determination. Once I understood what was going on in my head and realized that I was not 'stupid,' I figured out all sorts of ingenious ways to cope.

Jamie Janover. "Following Bliss." LDOnline Personal Stories. www.ldonline.org /firstperson/7019.

sequencing and perceive letters, numbers, and words in the wrong order. He might struggle to relate the specific ideas in a story to broader, more general ideas or to apply the concepts used in solving one math problem to solving similar problems. A disability at the integration step can also make it difficult to infer meaning and get the big-picture ideas in a story or even to understand the humor in the punch line of a joke.

Once the brain has made sense of the information, it is held in short-term memory, where it is stored and available until it is no longer needed. A person with a disability that interferes with "memory," the third step in the learning process, might not be able to hold the ten digits of a phone number in her mind while trying to call someone, or she might forget the words to a spelling list the day after she memorizes them.

In the final step of the learning process, the brain sends a message to the nerves and muscles to express the information as output. Output can take the form of writing, speaking, drawing, gesturing with the hands, or moving other muscles of the body. A learning disability in the output step might make it hard to communicate verbally or in writing. It might also interfere with the signals the brain sends to the muscles of the hand and fingers and make it difficult to form the letters of the alphabet.

A Look Inside the Brain

Inside the brain, the steps of the learning process do not look orderly at all. Learning involves billions of microscopic brain cells called neurons, the electrical signals that they constantly relay back and forth to each other, and the hundreds of chemicals that either stimulate the cells to send signals or inhibit them from doing so.

When babies are born, all of the neurons that they will ever have in their lifetimes are present in their brains, about 100 billion of them—as many as there are stars in the Milky Way. Yet most of these neurons are not active. As the baby grows and takes in sensory information from the outside world, neurons are activated and begin firing, sending out electrical signals or connections to other neurons. This, in turn, stimulates these neurons to fire and send electrical charges to other neurons, setting off a chain reaction until the message either reaches its destination or gets lost or interrupted along the way. Throughout childhood, adolescence, and into adulthood, the gaps between neurons are constantly being closed with "learning connections." This ensures that when the brain receives the same sensory information the next time around, it will respond more quickly, and the person thus learns from experience.

The process of neurons' firing and forming new learning connections takes place throughout the central cortex, or thinking part of the brain. The central cortex has four important roles. It controls language, muscle movement, cognition (thinking), and executive function (organization and planning tasks). It is divided into two hemispheres, left and right, each of which controls movement in the opposite side of the body and also specializes in different aspects of learning. The left hemisphere is heavily involved in processing and expressing language. The right hemisphere is dominant when the tasks are visual or nonverbal. Yet the regions of the cortex do not work in isolation. Making a decision about even the most trivial aspect of daily life, such as brushing teeth, for example, requires that different regions of the brain work together.

Differently Wired Brains

For decades, researchers assumed that learning disabilities had a neurological basis—that they were caused by structural differences in the brain and nervous system, such as faulty "wiring," or connections, between neurons. With advances in technology, they have been able to confirm that the brains of learning-disabled people are just wired a little differently. The first evidence came from autopsies conducted on the brain tissue of learning-disabled people after their deaths. Using a microscope to examine the cells in the tissue, researchers found clusters of neurons where they did not expect to see them. They also found neurons with loose extensions that branched out but never reached other neurons. Since the brains that were studied belonged to people who struggled with reading, the researchers were not surprised to discover these unusual patterns of neurons in the region of the brain that controls language. They concluded that these brains were not optimally wired for reading. They also found that while 65 percent of non-learning-disabled people have larger left hemispheres, the part of the brain that is most involved in language, people with reading disabilities are more likely to have larger right hemispheres—the area that is dominant in visual tasks—or to have brain hemispheres of equal size.

In the 1980s researchers began to use new imaging technologies such as magnetic resonance imaging (MRI) to better understand learning disabilities. MRI uses a powerful magnetic field and radio waves to detect changes in the magnetic properties of molecules in the body. It creates detailed pictures of the tissues of the brain and other organs. A newer technology called functional MRI (fMRI) creates images that show which areas of the brain are active as a person carries out a task such as reading or writing. When circuits of neurons are active, they consume more energy, and this in turn causes more blood to

Researchers began to use groundbreaking new brain imaging technologies such as magnetic resonance imaging (MRI, pictured) to better understand learning disabilities.

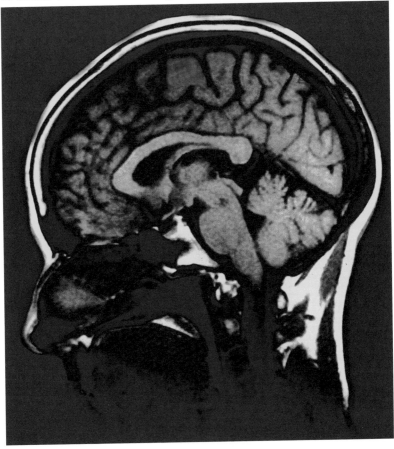

flow to the brain. Functional MRI detects the magnetic properties in the blood. In fMRI studies, researchers ask children to read or write and then map the pattern of the children's brain activity during each step in the reading process. They then compare these patterns in boys and girls with and without learning disabilities. These studies show that the patterns of activity in the brains of learning-disabled children during reading vary from that of their non-learning-disabled peers; further proof that their brains are wired a little differently.

These studies also reveal that the brain is extremely "plastic," or flexible. Learning connections continue to form between neurons throughout a person's lifetime. Interventions, such as intensive reading programs that help learning-disabled children learn the building blocks of reading, for example, have been shown to actually "rewire" the structure of the brain and change the way it responds to written language.

Learning Disabilities Run in Families

The new brain-imaging studies can reveal where a learning disability occurs, but they do not explain what causes a brain to be wired differently. The answer often lies in the genetic code. During pregnancy, the genes instruct the brain to wire itself differently. If a child's parent, sibling, or extended family member has a learning disability, there is a significantly higher-than-average chance that the child will have a disability, too. Yet although learning disabilities tend to run in families, the specific disability may take a slightly different form from parent to child. The parent may have a weakness in processing written language, while the child has a related but slightly different problem with written expression. This leads researchers to believe that it is not the specific learning disability that is inherited but a disturbance in brain structure that is passed on through the genes.

Studies of identical twins who were separated at birth confirm that genetics are a major cause of reading-related learning disabilities. The identical twins share a genetic code. Researchers have found that if one twin has a learning disability, the other twin also has a learning disability 68 percent of the time.

Boys Versus Girls

Do boys really have learning disabilities more often than girls? The student populations of the special education resource rooms of the 1970s were heavily dominated by boys. Even today, boys are nearly three times more likely than girls to be identified as learning disabled in schools. Although new studies reveal that there are gender differences in the structure of male and female brains, most researchers believe the gender gap is due to teacher bias. Boys who are struggling are often more disruptive in the classroom. They tend to have difficulty with skills such as handwriting or drawing that attract teachers' attention in the early grades. Girls who are having problems often respond by becoming quiet and withdrawing to avoid calling attention to themselves.

In a large-scale study of reading performance in Connecticut, researchers tested 445 children in kindergartens across the state and then followed the children through their school years. The researchers compared the children who met the criteria for reading disabilities in their research studies with the number of children with reading disabilities identified by the school system. The ratio of boys to girls identified in the school population was more than three to one. In contrast, in the researchers' studies, the ratio was closer to one to one—the number of boys and girls with reading-related disabilities was nearly identical.

Early special education resource rooms of the 1970s were heavily boy-dominated.

Environment Plays a Role

When there are no obvious genetic links for a child's learning disability, the causes can be harder to trace. Sometimes there are conditions during pregnancy that change the structure of

A health campaign ad poster showing a fetus in utero sends a strong message to pregnant women not to smoke. Maternal use of drugs, cigarettes, or alcohol during pregnancy is known to harm the developing brain and can lead to learning disabilities.

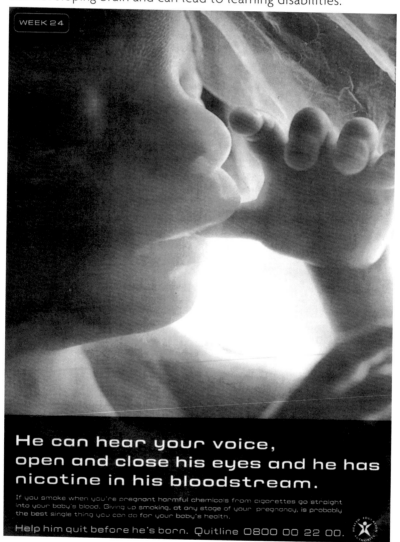

the developing brain. If the fetus lacks oxygen or nutrition or the mother is seriously ill or malnourished, the child may be born with learning problems. Maternal use of drugs, cigarettes, or alcohol during pregnancy is known to harm the developing brain and can lead to learning disabilities. Children who are born prematurely are also more prone to learning disabilities than those who reach full term in pregnancy, especially if they are born with a very low birth weight.

In other cases, there are problems in infancy or early childhood at a time when the brain is exploding with new learning connections. Children who experience a traumatic illness, such as very high, prolonged fever or injury to the head, can develop learning disabilities. Infants and young children are also especially susceptible to toxins present in the environment, such as lead, aluminum, and mercury. These toxins have been linked, or in the case of lead, proven to cause learning disabilities. Children are usually exposed to lead when they live in older homes with lead water pipes or peeling lead-based paint. Even low levels of lead have been found to have a major impact on the developing brain.

Some researchers believe that if children grow up in extreme deprivation and are not exposed to talk, laughter, play, and interaction with other human beings during a critical phase of development from birth to age four, they may develop learning disabilities. Others say that although neglect and emotional distress in childhood have a serious effect on learning and behavior, these can be addressed with the right interventions and do not necessarily rewire the brain.

Sometimes, there are no obvious genetic or environmental factors to explain a child's learning disability, but this uncertainty does not make the problems they face any less real.

Who Has a Learning Disability?

One thing that is certain about learning disabilities, they are very common. "Growing up," writes author and radio personality Nelson Lauver in his memoir *Most Unlikely to Succeed*, "I thought I was the only kid like me in the world. I thought I was all alone. Many years later, as my life changed for the better, I slowly came to understand that my story was, and is, the story of millions of Americans who struggle with literacy."[4]

According to the National Center for Learning Disabilities, it is likely that between 10 and 15 percent of Americans, or roughly one in every seven people, have a learning disability. Learning-disabled people belong to every race, ethnicity, and income level. They live in all regions of the country and the world, in rural towns, large cities, and wealthy suburbs. In U.S. schools, nearly 2.5 million students aged three to twenty-one, or more than 5 percent of students, are classified as having a specific learning disability and receive special education services. That number is probably much higher, because many children with learning disabilities are never identified in school. They may compensate and perform well enough to keep up with grade-level work, or, like Lauver, they may be written off as underachievers who are lazy or unmotivated. Some researchers suggest that learning-disabled students make up closer to 10 percent of all students in U.S. schools.

For many years the popular wisdom was that boys were more likely to have learning disabilities than girls. Recent research suggests that the number of boys and girls with learning disabilities is actually very similar.

What a Learning Disability Is Not

Not all children who struggle in school have a learning disability. Everyone learns and matures at a different rate. People also have different ways of learning. Some might study for a test by reading new vocabulary out loud, while others look at the words silently and commit them to memory. Some prefer to complete a long-term assignment by spreading the work out over several days, while others work more intensively and finish in one session. These are learning styles and preferences, but they are not learning disabilities.

Children who grow up in poverty or in immigrant families where English is not spoken at home have fewer chances to

Sometimes the media and the public confuse autism with learning disabilities. People with autism and other developmental disorders, like the boy pictured, experience difficulty with language, emotions, and social skills.

develop their vocabularies in childhood. They often struggle to learn to read or write when they reach school age. Being poor or disadvantaged can make it extremely challenging for students to achieve success in school, but it does not make these students learning disabled.

Sometimes the media and the public confuse autism and Asperger's syndrome with learning disabilities. People with these developmental disorders experience difficulty with language, emotions, and social skills. Although there is some overlap with the problems that learning-disabled and autistic children face, autism disorders are not learning disabilities.

For many years, children with learning disabilities were labeled as "mentally retarded," a term that has been used in such cruel and hurtful ways to insult people's intelligence that it has recently been replaced in schools and other settings by the term *intellectually disabled*. Children who are intellectually disabled perform significantly below the average range on a test of intelligence. To meet the criteria for a learning disability, a child must demonstrate average or above average intellectual capacity even if she is achieving below-grade-level expectations. The terms sound similar, but an intellectual disability is not a learning disability.

Over the years, there have been many ways in which learning-disabled children and adults have been mislabeled and misunderstood. This is because they are "unusual learners," says child psychiatrist Edward M. Hallowell. "The unusual learner is hard to teach, which makes him a target for name-calling. Stupid and bad are just two of the many words that have stung him for centuries. Wayward, slow, deviant, incorrigible, and many other essentially moral diagnoses have obscured what we are now, finally, discovering is a medical diagnosis. It turns out these kids—and the adults they become—have a lot to offer."[5]

CHAPTER TWO

Types of Learning Disabilities

A child in the second grade is intellectually curious and eager to take part in classroom activities but struggles to learn to read and write. His teacher suggests that he has "dyslexia." A psychologist evaluates his learning problems and labels his condition a "language-based learning disability," while a speech and language therapist who meets with him determines that he has an "auditory processing deficit."

There are many different labels used to describe the types of disabilities that interfere with learning. This can lead to confusion when professionals with different backgrounds and expertise use different terms to describe similar or overlapping conditions. In many cases, teachers are the first to identify children with learning disabilities in the early years of elementary school. Labels like "dyslexia" (difficulty with reading) and "dyscalculia" (trouble with math) are widely used as a way of describing the challenges students face in academic subject areas. Yet learning disabilities rarely fit into neat academic categories. Children who have a disability that interferes with their understanding of written language may also struggle when they listen to a lecture or try to interpret the language of a math problem because these draw on the same circuits of neurons in the brain.

As the understanding of the brain has evolved, educators have begun to look beyond labels to ask where in the learning process a breakdown occurs, whether in input, integration (or processing), memory, or output. If they observe a weakness in one area of learning, they also want to know whether a child has a corresponding strength in another area. "Even though an educational difficulty can be labeled," researchers warn, "labeling rarely leads to universal success as the polio vaccine did in the field of medicine."[6] When it comes to learning disabilities, there is no one-size-fits-all approach.

Language-Based Learning Disabilities

Many students with dyslexia describe a feeling of dread when it is time to read aloud in class. They hope and pray that they will not be called on. They slouch in their chairs, hide their faces, or raise their hands to go to the bathroom where they count the seconds until reading time is over. In *Faking It*, his memoir of growing up with severe dyslexia, Christopher Lee tells of the terror he felt at being called on by his teacher to read aloud. "I don't know if I was scared or embarrassed or hurt or a mixture of all three, but I couldn't speak. I could not say one word. The whole class was staring at me. I could not read what was on the board, and I could not come up with a lie. I was faced with a classroom full of kids watching me fail, and realized that I could no longer hide the fact that I was stupid."[7]

The word *dyslexia* comes from the Greek words *dys*, meaning poor or difficulty with, and *lexis*, meaning word or language. It is widely used to describe a learning disability that causes difficulty with reading, spelling, and writing. Children and adults with dyslexia struggle to recognize and decode written words. They read slowly and inaccurately and often have poor spelling. They may also skip words or entire lines of text and have difficulty staying focused on the material. Dyslexia is fairly common. A Yale University study on reading performance that followed 445 students through their school years in the state of Connecticut found that as many as 1 out of every 5 of the students showed some signs of dyslexia. Other studies suggest that the condition is just as prevalent in non-English-speaking parts of the world, although in countries such as China that use pictographs for reading and writing, different regions of the brain may be affected.

For many years, researchers assumed that dyslexia was linked to problems in the way the brain processes visual information. This is because dyslexia is most often associated with so-called mirror reading, reversing the letters of a word or reading a word backwards. This is a misconception. The idea of a visual link to

Children and adults with dyslexia struggle to recognize and decode words.

dyslexia has been slow to fade away in the popular culture, but researchers have found no evidence to suggest that dyslexics actually see words or letters backwards. In fact, many children write backwards in the early stages of learning to read and write.

Instead, research on the brain has shown that dyslexia is linked to a breakdown in the auditory processing and sequencing phase of the learning process. People with dyslexia have trouble breaking down words into the smallest separate units of sound, called phonemes; putting these sounds together to form words; and connecting the sounds to written letters. Educators call this group of skills "phonological awareness." Dyslexics also struggle to retrieve the sounds of letters and words from memory and apply this to new words or to recall familiar words. When a child who is learning to read sees the letters d-o-g, for example, she retrieves the sounds for those letters from memory and then blends the sounds and reads the word dog.

Many of the same auditory-processing skills are crucial not only in reading but also in other areas of language learning. People who are dyslexic may have trouble with writing, spelling, memorizing and recalling vocabulary, following verbal instructions, or communicating clearly. Educators often use the term *language-based learning disabilities* to refer to all of these difficulties in receiving, processing, and expressing written or oral language. As many as 80 percent of those identified in school as having a learning disability have a language-based learning disability.

Dysgraphia and Written Language Disabilities

Dysgraphia, or difficulty with writing, also falls under language-based learning disabilities. It is a disability in written language and expression.

People with dysgraphia typically have messy, illegible handwriting. Lee says in *Faking It* that writing is his "worst nightmare." "I never know if anything I'm writing is correct; stopping and starting, I am constantly trying to figure out how to form the next letter or to decide what the next letter should

Creative Visual Thinkers

According to Thomas G. West, author of *In the Mind's Eye*, some of the world's greatest scientists, artists, mathematicians, political leaders, and poets would probably have been diagnosed with dyslexia if they were alive today. West explains that visionaries like inventor Thomas Edison, physicist Albert Einstein, and artist Leonardo da Vinci had a remarkable ability to think in pictures. Yet their heightened visual-spatial imaginations came at a cost. "They may have been so much in touch with their visual-spatial, nonverbal, right hemisphere modes of thought," West writes, "that they have had difficulty in doing orderly, sequential, verbal-mathematical, left-hemisphere tasks." Most struggled in their early school years with tasks that involved verbal skills or short-term memory, such as reading, spelling, and retaining math facts.

In the Mind's Eye has been influential in changing the way people think about dyslexia. West does not argue that these great thinkers learned to compensate for their disabilities nor that they were more motivated than others to overcome the challenges they faced. Instead, he says, they succeeded because they could *not* fully compensate. Their "disabilities," or differences in the way their brains were wired, are what allowed them to have great insights and to accomplish extraordinary things.

Thomas G. West. *In the Mind's Eye: Creative Visual Thinkers, Gifted Dyslexics, and the Rise of Visual Technologies.* Amherst, NY: Prometheus, 2009, p. 32.

Many visionary visual thinkers, like Leonardo da Vinci, struggled in their early years with tasks that involved verbal skills or short-term memory, such as reading, spelling, and retaining math facts.

be. . . . Words never seem to be spelled the way I hear them, and they never look the same way twice."[8]

Like reading, writing is a complicated process. Dysgraphia can be caused by a breakdown at any one or more of the steps of learning, including processing and sequencing, memory, or output and expression. People who have difficulty sequencing and organizing auditory information, including those with dyslexia, may find it difficult to recall the order of letters and words as they write and need to slow way down to write correctly. Or they may experience extreme difficulty with the mechanics of spelling and punctuation. When dysgraphia is linked to fine motor output or expression, there is a problem in the way the brain relays messages to coordinate the muscles of the dominant hand. People who are dysgraphic often complain that their hands cannot work as fast as their minds are thinking. Even filling in the blanks on a school form or job application with personal information such as name and address can turn into a painstaking process.

Some people with dysgraphia also have trouble with written expression. They become so bogged down in the mechanics of writing that they lose sight of the big-picture ideas they want to express. They often describe staring hopelessly at a blank page for minutes or even hours, unable to let their ideas stream from their heads onto the paper. In many cases, typing on a computer keyboard frees them to express themselves more effectively.

Fine and Gross Motor Disabilities

Some people with dysgraphia struggle with the mechanics of writing because they cannot make the muscles in their dominant hand work together. This is a fine motor disability, also referred to as developmental coordination disorder or dyspraxia (from the Greek word *praxia*, meaning movement). It can interfere with any tasks that involve the coordination of groups of fine or small muscles, including cutting with scissors, tying shoes, coloring within the lines of a drawing, buttoning a shirt, or typing. People with dyspraxia have to concentrate on the movements their fingers and hands are making while they

Dyspraxia can interfere with any tasks that involve the coordination of groups of fine or small muscles, such as cutting with scissors.

are writing, cutting, or drawing in order to effectively complete such a task.

Sometimes dyspraxia affects gross motor skills, or the co-ordination of larger muscle groups. People who have a gross motor disability often appear clumsy and bump into things, or have trouble with physical activities like running or climbing, or with activities that require eye-hand coordination, such as

Living with Severe Dyscalculia

"I am twenty-five years old and I can't tell time. I struggle with dialing phone numbers, counting money, balancing my checkbook, tipping at restaurants, following directions, understanding distances, and applying basic math to my everyday life. I also struggle with spelling and grammar, and remembering combinations of movements in athletics and dance. I cannot read a note of music."

This is how Samantha Abeel introduces her memoir, *My Thirteenth Winter*, in which she recounts the pain and frustration of growing up with severe dyscalculia. As a young child, Abeel was enthusiastic and curious. She laughed easily and was eager to learn. Within weeks of starting kindergarten, however, she realized she was different. She managed to earn good grades because of her strong verbal abilities and hard work. Yet a life spent trying to hide her disability weighed heavily on her. By high school, she began to feel anxious and depressed. She was lost until a teacher recognized the power and beauty of her writing. She published her first book of poetry at age fifteen. Although depression and anxiety continued to plague her through her college years, Abeel finally found healing when she learned to accept her disability as a "rather strange and unusual gift" that enabled her to reach out and help others.

Samantha Abeel. *My Thirteenth Winter: A Memoir*. New York: Scholastic, 2003, pp. 1, 201.

hitting a baseball with a bat. As adults, they may struggle with routine tasks such as driving, cooking, or shaving. In some cases, dyspraxia interferes with the ability to speak, because the areas of the brain that control hand and mouth movements are close together in the brain's central cortex.

Researchers believe that both fine and gross motor disabilities are most often caused by a problem in the output phase of the learning process. In order to run, jump, or write, the brain has to convey messages to the nerves and muscles to complete the action. A motor disability may also involve visual processing. In this case, the person processes visual or spatial information poorly and relays information to the muscles incorrectly during activities like catching a ball or jumping rope.

Math and Numerical Disabilities

Visual processing is often at the heart of another type of learning disability: dyscalculia, meaning difficulty with math, which causes profound difficulty solving math problems or grasping numerical relationships. There is a lot of confusion around dyscalculia, because it covers such a wide range of math-related difficulties. Students may have trouble understanding the meaning and magnitude of numbers. Or they may have a sequencing issue and have trouble organizing the information required to solve a math problem. They may also struggle with the language of math or have short-term memory deficits that prevent them from memorizing and retrieving math facts and formulas. One of the most common causes of math disability is a visual processing weakness that makes it difficult for people to visualize numbers and math situations as they apply to time, distance, space, and other abstract concepts. Even as a middle school student, Samantha Abeel, author of a memoir for young adults titled *My Thirteenth Winter*, was a gifted young writer, but she could not grasp basic math skills. "While I could recite the numbers and the multiplication tables that I had memorized, they were only symbols with numerical names that didn't mean anything to me. I didn't understand the concepts behind them,"[9] she writes.

Researchers believe that math disabilities are nearly as common as language-based disabilities, but they often go undetected. In most schools, students must fall far behind their classmates in math before they are labeled with a learning disability. This is because many non-learning-disabled students struggle with one or more aspects of math, too. Many also develop math phobias because of a negative experience in a math class or a lack of self-confidence. This makes it harder to recognize when a child's math problems stem from a disability.

Yet there is a high price to pay when students fail to build a solid math foundation early in their school years. They often become lost and confused when confronted with more complex, multistep equations and problems in high school. As adults, they become overwhelmed when they need to figure out grocery costs, leave a tip, create a budget, estimate time and distance, or make financial decisions that affect their lives.

Nonverbal Learning Disabilities

While dyscalculia can be caused by a breakdown in visual-processing skills, people with nonverbal learning disability have a more widespread visual- and spatial-processing weakness. They struggle with math operations that involve visual-spatial memory, such as borrowing in a subtraction problem or solving for a variable in algebra. They also have difficulty reading a map, chart, or graph and engaging in hands-on activities such as science labs and arts and crafts projects. They lack coordination, balance, and a sense of direction. In contrast to a language-based learning disability, which is often thought of as a disability of the left hemisphere of the brain, which is dominant in verbal tasks, a nonverbal learning disability is a disability of the right hemisphere, the hemisphere dominant in tasks that involve visual and spatial skills.

In fact, people with nonverbal learning disabilities tend to have exceptional verbal skills and are sometimes labeled as "gifted" in school. Tera Kirk was an extremely verbal child. She spoke her first words at the age of seven months and was reading the encyclopedia by the second grade. Yet she often became lost and disoriented when trying to find her classroom. "Sometimes it's as though I see things in pieces—I break rooms and objects down into simple visual bits, like colors. In first grade, I went to class in what I thought of as a 'White Room.' It had white walls and a carpet that only seemed to accentuate their whiteness. I know a room by the color of the walls or of the floor, rarely both at once."[10]

Some people with nonverbal learning disabilities are also awkward in social situations. They fail to interpret nonverbal cues such as facial expression, gestures, and body language, or they misread important social cues and have a hard time making and keeping friends.

The Role of Executive Function

Both nonverbal and language-based learning disabilities are often accompanied by a weakness in executive function. This term is used to describe the set of mental processes that people use to regulate behaviors and accomplish a task. Executive function is compared to the conductor of an orchestra, the CEO of a

Executive function is compared to the conductor of an orchestra. It is involved in planning, monitoring, organizing, evaluating, and adjusting course as needed.

company, or the traffic controller at a busy airport, who directs planes to take off and land, tracks stormy weather, and ensures that passengers and luggage arrive safely at their destinations. Executive function is involved in planning, monitoring, organizing, evaluating, and adjusting course as needed to get a job done. Executive function plays a role when the task is simple, such as throwing a ball or picking up a pencil, or more complex, such as searching the Internet for information or driving a car.

Learning-disabled people who also have executive function weakness struggle to stay organized and carry out tasks in a timely and efficient way. They may have trouble starting a project or estimating how long it will take. They may find it difficult to come up with ideas independently or to tell a story from start to finish without getting lost in the details. They often lack motivation to finish a task, especially when it seems difficult or frustrating. They may also struggle to retain information in working memory for long enough to make use of it; for example, holding onto the words at the beginning of this sentence until they reach the end.

The idea of executive function is widely used and accepted by researchers, but it is more of a theory than something that is easily measured or defined. In fact, problems with executive function seem to overlap with or are a feature of many other types of learning disabilities. Researchers believe that as the brain matures and forms new learning connections, executive function changes and develops, too. This process can be helped along when children are directly taught to organize, plan, and self-monitor their behaviors.

ADHD and Learning Disabilities

Attention deficit disorder (ADD) and attention deficit/ hyperactivity disorder (ADHD) are behavioral conditions that are also closely linked to learning disabilities. ADD or ADHD co-occurs with learning disabilities in nearly one-third of the children who receive special education services in school. Children with ADD or ADHD tend to get noticed. They are often hyperactive, easily distracted, and impulsive. They fidget in

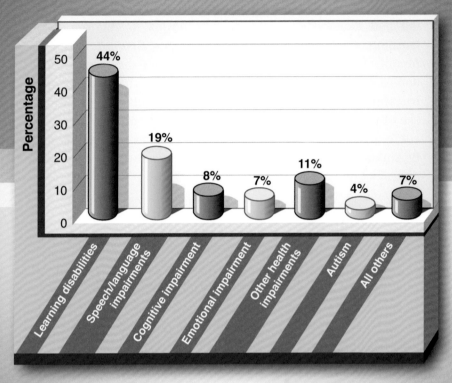

Special Education Students by Disability Category, 2007

Percentage

50 — 44%
40
30 — 19%
20 — 8% 7% 11%
10 — 4% 7%
0

Learning disabilities
Speech/language impairments
Cognitive impairment
Emotional impairment
Other health impairments
Autism
All others

Taken from: 2007 Child Count. www.IDEAdata.org.

their seats, interrupt, lose their belongings, or talk incessantly, all of which are disruptive behaviors that are hard for teachers to ignore in the classroom.

Researchers believe that ADD and ADHD are caused by a disruption in connections between neurons in the brain. One of the differences between ADD or ADHD and a learning disability is that these connections extend beyond the central cortex to circuits of neurons that are known collectively as the "area of vigilance." The area of vigilance is believed to have been associated with the qualities that made early humans such effective hunters. It allowed them to track prey without getting distracted by the sights or sounds around them, wait patiently, and then strike at exactly the right moment.

Although the terms were not widely used until the 1980s, ADD and ADHD have since become the most frequently studied and diagnosed psychiatric conditions in children. Like learning disabilities, they are conditions that often run in families and are lifelong. Yet, unlike learning disabilities, ADD and ADHD are often treated with medication that helps people to calm down and focus their attention. While the conditions are often associated with negative behaviors in the classroom, some researchers have begun to ask whether they might also be linked to positive attributes such as creativity, entrepreneurship, and innovative, or "outside the box," thinking.

Related Behavior and Emotional Issues

Even when ADD or ADHD is not a factor, learning disabilities and behavioral or emotional problems often go hand in hand. Learning-disabled students usually have to work harder than their peers do to succeed. They tend to receive more negative feedback from teachers and classmates. When rated by their peers and teachers, they are often seen as less socially acceptable than are other students. Many learning-disabled children exhibit emotional and behavioral problems that grow out of their frustrations and anxieties as they struggle to learn and to fit in. It is easier to attract attention as the class clown who always makes other students laugh than to feel stupid or left behind, or to threaten and tease other students than to become a victim of teasing and bullying. In his memoir *Most Unlikely to Succeed*, Nelson Lauver describes a pivotal moment in the third grade when a teacher humiliated him in front of the class for his messy handwriting. He decided that the only way to earn the respect of his peers was to adopt a bad attitude. "I said to myself, Nelson, you have a choice. You can either look like the dumb kid who everyone makes fun of, or you can be the bad kid. At that moment, I chose to be the 'bad kid.' The thought of being the 'dumb kid' and how other kids teased and taunted them—made it feel like the only choice."[11]

Low expectations and low self-esteem take a heavy toll on many learning-disabled children. By the time they enter high

Low expectations and self-esteem take a heavy toll on many learning-disabled children. They are more likely than their non-learning disabled peers to encounter trouble with the law and end up in the juvenile justice system.

school, they have experienced so much failure that many reject the school environment altogether. Estimates suggest that students with learning disabilities drop out of high school at more than twice the rate of their non-learning-disabled peers. They are also far more likely to turn to drugs and alcohol or to get into trouble with the law and end up in the juvenile justice system. As adults, they experience high rates of depression, poverty, and long-term unemployment.

In fact, for people with learning disabilities, emotional problems such as anger, frustration, and low self-esteem are often as much of a barrier to success as their academic weaknesses. When these issues are not addressed in childhood, they can lead to a lifetime of painful and damaging behaviors. "Amazingly, I learned that dyslexia had not necessarily been my greatest impediment to learning to read and write," Lauver explains. "Anger, guilt, fear, and blame held me back as much as the learning disability itself."[12]

CHAPTER THREE

The History of Learning Disabilities

In *Legacy of the Blue Heron*, Harry Sylvester's memoir of growing up in the 1930s and 1940s, describes the harsh measures that teachers used to try to force learning-disabled children to read and write in school. "They [the learning disabled] were put in a storeroom with a book and told not to come out until they could read; they were put in a cloakroom away from the rest of the class and told not to disturb anybody; or they were told to go down in the basement and spend their days with the janitor."[13] Sylvester himself spent hours standing alone in the hallway, or sitting in the classroom at recess with his unfinished workbook, listening to the sounds of his classmates as they laughed and played outside.

From the earliest days of public education, children with learning disabilities suffered misunderstanding and mistreatment in schools. For decades, they were labeled as brain-damaged, mentally retarded, lazy, or unmotivated. They were punished, humiliated, and bullied by teachers and classmates. Until the 1970s they were likely to be separated from their peers and placed in isolated classrooms with children who were intellectually or physically disabled, or who had severe behavioral and emotional problems. It was not uncommon for a child with a learning disability to be held back in school until he had outgrown the desks and chairs. Most never graduated from high school or dreamed of pursuing a college degree.

Researchers studied children and adults with reading and writing difficulties as early as the nineteenth century, and published their findings in scientific and professional journals. They used a variety of labels such as *brain-damaged* and *word-blind* in an attempt to explain what they observed. Some noted that their subjects were intelligent, even though they often had low IQ scores or struggled to learn basic skills. Others worked to develop new methods of instruction to support children with learning difficulty, but for years their efforts had little impact in the public schools.

In the 1960s and 1970s, life for people with learning disabilities finally began to change for the better. Spurred on by the civil rights movement, a growing disability rights movement began to take shape. The U.S. government passed new laws and policies to protect learning-disabled people from discrimination in schools, jobs, housing, and other areas of life. Slowly, over many years, public attitudes began to change, too.

Early Research on Language Disabilities

Learning disabilities first came to public attention in Europe in the late nineteenth century when physicians published accounts in the medical journals of the day. A Scottish eye doctor named James Hinshelwood reported at least a dozen cases of patients with an inherited condition that he called "word blindness," and which later become known as dyslexia. Like many researchers after him, Hinshelwood mistakenly assumed that dyslexia was linked to impaired visual perception. Yet he also had many insights about how to help his patients that were ahead of his time. He wanted to spare children the pain of being ridiculed and bullied in school and suggested that if their condition was recognized early enough, it could be remedied with intensive one-on-one instruction.

By the 1920s, U.S. clinicians and researchers also observed children with reading and writing difficulties and concluded, like Hinshelwood, that conventional methods of instruction in the schools were failing them. Samuel Orton was one of the key figures of this era to advance understanding of reading and language disabilities. Orton was a "neuropathologist" who

Late nineteenth-century researchers first concluded that students who experienced difficulty with reading and writing benefited from intensive one-on-one instruction.

worked with brain-damaged patients in a state-run psychiatric hospital in Iowa City, Iowa. He set up a mobile clinic in rural Iowa and invited local teachers to refer students who had been labeled, in the language of the era, as "defective" or "retarded." Orton observed the children as they read and administered a test of intelligence to determine IQ. He found that many of the children who had been labeled "retarded" actually scored in the average or above average range on the IQ test. The children who struggled with reading often had low scores, but Orton believed that these did not reflect their true intellectual capacity.

In later years Orton conducted further research with dyslexic children who seemed to reverse letters such as b and d and words such as *dog* and *god*. At the time, the inner workings of the brain were poorly understood. He attributed the children's difficulties to what he called a lack of cerebral dominance, the failure of one hemisphere of the brain to establish dominance over the other. Although his theory was eventually discredited, he too was ahead of his time in his belief that the reading problems he observed could be traced to connections inside the brain.

Pioneers of Reading Instruction

Orton also played an important role in developing reading instruction for children with dyslexia. He grew disillusioned with the "look-say" method widely used in the public schools of his day, and its emphasis on reading and memorizing words by sight. Orton was one of the first to advocate the step-by-step teaching of phonics, or letter-sound relationships, to children who had trouble learning to read.

Orton, along with contemporaries such as Anna Gillingham, Bessie Stillman, and Grace Fernald, pioneered new methods of reading instruction to help struggling readers. Many of these pioneering educators were women. At a time when other areas of research and science were often closed to them, women made key contributions to the field of education. They designed new methods of reading instruction, many of which are still in use today. These methods differ in style and substance, but share a strong focus on making reading a "multisensory" experience that involves visual, auditory, and kinesthetic, or movement-based, skills. Students speak words out loud, write words as they read them, and trace the letters with their fingers as they speak them. In contrast to attitudes prevalent in the public schools of the day, these reading instruction pioneers put the blame for students' failure to learn on flawed methods of instruction rather than on students. They believed that all children could learn to read if they were taught effectively. As Grace Fernald wrote in 1943, "Since no abilities are required for the mastery of reading, writing, and arithmetic which are not already possessed by the ordinary, normal individual, it seems obvious that there is no such thing as a person of normal intelligence who cannot learn these basic skills."[14]

A teacher instructs her students in phonics using the "look-say" method.

The Theory of Minimal Brain Damage

Even with advances in reading instruction, learning disabilities were still not well understood. In the early 1940s a new theory emerged to explain why some children who seemed intelligent might struggle to learn basic skills. Researchers observed that these children exhibited similar behaviors to people who had suffered brain damage after trauma to the head or brain surgery. They concluded that the children must have brain damage, too. Yet because the damage was not visible to the naked eye, it was believed to be minimal. The term *minimal brain damage* was widely used for more than a decade, along with terms such as *perceptually handicapped* and *brain injured,* to describe children with learning difficulties.

The theory of minimal brain damage finally fell out of favor in the 1950s, long after observations and testing failed to show any evidence for it. Researchers revised their thinking and proposed instead that children's learning difficulties must stem from problems with brain functioning. The term *minimal brain damage* was replaced by *minimal brain dysfunction syndrome,* with the word *dysfunction* included to suggest that something was faulty in the way the children's brains worked. The new theory came much closer to describing the differences in connections between neurons that scientists would observe in learning-disabled people many years later using advanced magnetic resonance imaging (MRI) and other imaging technologies. Yet the label *minimal brain dysfunction,* like *minimal brain damage,* reinforced negative stereotypes and implied that people were defective or broken. For decades, these labels influenced the way that teachers, parents, and classmates viewed learning-disabled children. They also had a profoundly negative effect on the way the children saw themselves.

A New Category of Disability Emerges

As early as the 1930s, there were some people in the research and education communities who rejected labels such as *minimally brain damaged* and *mentally retarded,* and challenged the common practice of separating children with learning difficulties from their peers. For years they were lone voices calling for change—until the evidence in support of their views could no longer be ignored.

Among the critics, some researchers questioned whether it was valid to use a single IQ test to measure intelligence and label children. Samuel Kirk, sometimes called the father of special education, was one of these critics. Kirk was a prominent psychologist who strongly objected to the practice of labeling and defining students with terms such as *mentally retarded* and *dyslexic.* He believed these labels created lowered expectations and limited children's potential for success in school and in life. Yet he is also credited as the first to introduce a new label, *learning disability*, to describe children who struggled to learn basic skills.

Kirk began his research in psychology in the 1920s at a residential facility in Chicago for delinquent boys who had been identified as mentally retarded. He grew intrigued by a ten-year-old boy at the facility who was diagnosed with "word blindness." Secretly, against the strict rules in place at the facility, he arranged to teach the boy to read. After seven months of intensive instruction, the boy was reading at a third-grade level and was released from the facility to attend regular school. The experience left a lasting impression on Kirk, who came to believe that children with disabilities could be successfully educated as long as they had the right early opportunities and classroom modifications. During a long and distinguished career, he developed ways of evaluating learning disabilities and worked for the passage of laws to guarantee that disabled students would be educated in the regular classroom.

Kirk's use of the term *learning disability* and its widespread acceptance as a new category of disability had a huge impact on American schools. He introduced the new term in a speech to a group of parents in 1963: "Recently, I have used the term 'learning disabilities' to describe a group of children who have disorders in development in language, speech, reading, and associated communication skills needed for social interaction."[15] Within just a few years of introducing the new term, demand for special education services climbed steeply. *Learning disability* soon became the most common category of disability among students referred for special education in U.S. public schools.

A Crisis in Special Education

The broadening of the term *disability* to include the category of learning disability created growing demand for support services in schools. Yet there was also another force at work that led to a dramatic rethinking of special education. In 1954

The Difficulty of Measuring Intelligence

Even Alfred Binet, the French psychologist who created the first IQ test in 1905, would have been surprised at the enthusiasm for his test in America. Binet devised a formula for calculating a child's mental age in comparison with his chronological age, which became known as an intelligence quotient, or IQ. He arrived at this measure by asking "average" French schoolchildren to answer a series of questions and comparing their performances with those of so-called mentally handicapped children of the same age. Although he was a strong proponent of testing, he warned that his IQ test was not a measure of inborn, or fixed, intelligence.

In the United States the Stanford-Binet IQ test first gained acceptance during World War I, when U.S. Army psychologists used it to sort thousands of soldiers who had been drafted into wartime service. After the war, it was adopted by the public schools to track students into different levels of instruction.

From the start, there were critics. In the 1920s Samuel Orton suggested that the test was badly suited for children with language

disabilities, because the questions were mainly verbal (modern tests aim for a balance between verbal and nonverbal questions). The test also raised concerns about racial and cultural bias, since it was used to track many poor and minority students into separate classrooms.

Alfred Binet was a French psychologist who created the first IQ test in 1905.

The Stanford-Binet IQ test (pictured) was determined to be
culturally biased.

the U.S. Supreme Court ruled, in a historic decision known in
short as *Brown v. Board of Education*, that state laws estab-
lishing separate public schools for black and white students
were unconstitutional. This was an era of deep-seated racism,
and parents and teachers in many school districts reacted
to the decision with alarm. They feared that white families
would flee urban school districts and move to the suburbs if
schools became racially integrated. (This is in fact what happened in many cities.) One way that some schools devised
to comply with the ruling while still managing to keep black

and white students segregated was to increase the use of IQ testing to track students into separate classrooms. In Washington, D.C., for example, between 1955 and 1956, the year immediately following the *Brown* ruling, enrollment doubled in special education classes. Of the students enrolled in these classes, more than three-fourths were African American, and most of these students were labeled either mentally retarded or emotionally disturbed.

This practice was repeated in school districts across the nation, where large numbers of poor and minority students were tracked into remedial and special education classrooms. In 1961 a young teacher in San Diego, California, named Barbara Lieber was assigned to a so-called upper special education class for students in the fourth through sixth grades. The students in the class were African American and Latino children from low-income neighborhoods of the city. Lieber recalls,

> I quickly discovered that all of the students could learn and they all became beginning or average readers at some level. Yet there were low or no expectations for them based on their performance on an intelligence test. Several years later, studies showed that the Stanford-Binet IQ test was a culturally biased test. It was found that if young children lacked background experiences to bring to the reading process they would not be as successful as others. If a child has never been to a zoo or heard of a giraffe, it is difficult to read a story about a giraffe.[16]

In the late 1960s, as educators called attention to the disturbing link between disability, poverty, and race, academic tracking in schools become the subject of intense controversy. In a highly influential article in 1968, an educator named Lloyd Dunn condemned the use of IQ tests to mislabel students, many of them racial minorities, and track them into isolated special education settings where they received an inferior education. "In my view, much of our past and present practices are morally and educationally wrong," he wrote. "We cannot ignore the evidence that removing a handicapped child from the regular grades for special education probably contributes significantly to his feelings of inferiority and problems of acceptance."[17]

The Disability Rights Movement

In the 1960s the calls for an overhaul of special education began with educators like Dunn but soon became part of a larger set of public demands to improve life for people with disabilities. Spurred on by the civil rights and women's liberation movements, disability rights groups formed across the nation. The movement started with efforts to protect the rights of the mentally retarded but quickly spread to those with a wide range of disabilities, from cerebral palsy to hearing impairment.

People with learning disabilities joined the larger movement for disability rights in 1963, when a group of concerned parents whose children struggled to read convened a meeting in Chicago. The parents argued that their children were not retarded, perceptually handicapped, or brain damaged and that these labels were damaging to their self-esteem. Kirk attended the meeting and delivered the speech in which he introduced the parents to the term *learning disability*. The parents founded a group that eventually became the Learning Disabilities Association of America to advocate on behalf of their children and pressure schools and government to improve special education services.

Educators slowly began to respond to the parents' demands. In schools across the country, special education services expanded. In some districts schools began to "mainstream" students with mild to moderate learning disabilities into general education classrooms for a greater portion of the school day, while also offering them support in special education resource rooms. Despite this progress, schools at this time were still under no legal obligation to provide services for learning-disabled students, and the quality of special education varied widely between cities and within school districts. In some schools there were no support services available at all, and students were left to falter or fail.

A Free and Appropriate Education for All

In 1975 the disability rights movement achieved a historic victory when the U.S. Congress passed public law 94-142, known at the time as the Education for All Handicapped Children Act. The new law stated that schools would not be eligible for federal funding unless they guaranteed that all disabled students between the ages of three and twenty-one receive a "free appropriate public education" in which they were educated alongside their nondisabled peers "to the maximum extent possible"[18] Children identified as having learning and other disabilities were to be mainstreamed into the general education classroom, unless teachers could prove that their disabilities were too severe to benefit from this change. Disabled students were also entitled to receive support services from trained resource specialists assigned to each school.

The 1975 law was a huge step in reversing decades of mistreatment. Yet within a few years of its passage, schools were overwhelmed by the demand for services. The government had vastly underestimated the number of children who would be identified as having learning disabilities, as well as the expense of evaluating and providing special education services for them. Many teachers were unprepared for the changes and did little to modify their instruction for the disabled students who joined their classes. Learning-disabled students not only struggled and fell behind their peers in the regular classroom, but also grew discouraged by the poor quality of instruction they received in the resource room. In the late 1970s Lynn, a student with dyslexia, was one of the only girls in her school to attend special sessions in the resource room. "I did not have one positive feeling about that room," she recalls. "I would do what they told me to do, recite what they told me to recite, but I was rarely asked to really think, and I almost

The Americans with Disabilities Act (being signed by George H.W. Bush in the picture) guarantees learning-disabled children and adults equal access not only to schools, but also to workplaces, housing, and public services.

never experienced those moments when something I was learning came together and made sense."[19]

For years parents and teacher groups complained about the lack of skilled teachers and instruction for disabled students like Lynn. The U.S. Congress finally responded in 1990 by expanding and revising the 1975 law to provide states with more federal funding and resources for special education. The name of the law was changed to the Individuals with Disabilities Education Act (IDEA). IDEA has been revised and amended in the years since, but the goal of the law remains the same: to protect disabled students from discrimination and ensure that they are educated to the greatest extent possible in the regular classroom alongside their nondisabled peers.

The Idea of IDEA: Protecting Students with Disabilities

The passage of the Education for All Handicapped Children Act, later renamed the Individuals with Disabilities Education Act (IDEA), set the stage for dramatic changes in public education. Before the law was passed, fewer than half of all U.S. children with known disabilities received a public or private school education. The law opened doors to children who had been barred by state laws from attending school. It also improved the quality of education for children with disabilities who were already part of the public school system. This included children with learning disabilities, who had been mistreated or isolated in special education classrooms for decades. The law required that schools provide "a free and appropriate public education" for every child, regardless of their disability.

IDEA also established standards for the way that children with disabilities were to be educated. It entitled every child with special needs to an evaluation by a team of professionals and allowed the child and his parents to take an active role in decisions about classroom placement and learning. IDEA is sometimes called the "mainstreaming law" because it requires that children with disabilities be educated alongside their peers in the "least restrictive environment." For some disabled children, this meant that they became part of the regular education classroom for the first time.

Percentage of Youth Ages 3–21 in Early Education Centers or Public Schools Receiving Services Under the Individuals with Disabilities Education Act (IDEA), by Primary Disability Type: Selected Years, 1976–1977 through 2005–2006

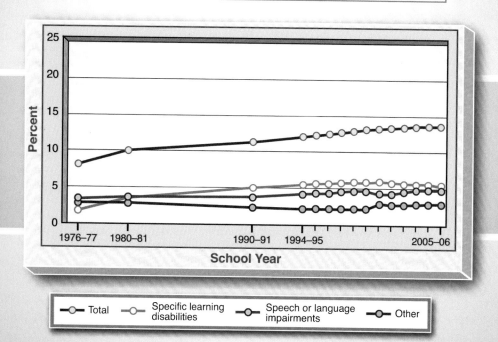

Taken from: U.S. Department of Education, National Center for Education Statistics.
www.aim.cast.org/learn/practice/use/accessible–TextboksII.

In the years since the 1975 law was passed, other changes have been made in an effort to improve the school experience for students with learning disabilities. In many schools, mainstreaming has slowly been replaced by the idea of "inclusion," in which classroom teachers teach side by side with special educators to address the needs of learning-disabled students, and even children with severe disabilities are included and spend some time during the day in the regular classroom.

New laws have also been passed, including the historic civil rights law the Americans with Disabilities Act (ADA), which guarantees learning-disabled children and adults equal access not only to schools but also to workplaces, housing, and public services. While many challenges remain, laws and policies such as IDEA, have enhanced the quality of life and access to education for tens of millions of children and adults with learning disabilities.

CHAPTER FOUR

Learning Disabilities in School

In 1975 President Gerald Ford signed the historic Education for All Handicapped Children bill into law (which later became IDEA). "Everyone can agree with the objective stated in the title of this bill, educating all handicapped children in our Nation," Ford declared during the signing ceremony. Yet the president also expressed deep reservations about whether public schools could deliver on the law's provisions, since these would require increased government spending to support children with a wide range of disabilities. "The key question," he went on, "is whether the bill will really accomplish this objective."[20]

U.S. schools have made great strides since the days when students were excluded or ridiculed and bullied for failing to perform. Since the passage of IDEA in 1975, every child with a disability has been entitled to a "free and appropriate education." Many schools teach children to be tolerant and respectful of people who look or learn differently. Some also make a commitment to so-called inclusion classrooms, in which regular teachers collaborate closely with special educators, and students of diverse backgrounds and abilities work together.

Yet for many learning-disabled students, schools remain difficult places. IDEA ensured that they would be educated alongside their nondisabled peers, but the law does not always result in better learning experiences or full inclusion in the school community.

Few people would suggest turning back the clock to an earlier era, but many have begun to ask whether a new approach to special education is needed to ensure that children with learning disabilities can participate fully in school and life.

In 1975 President Gerald Ford (pictured) signed the historic Education for All Handicapped Children bill into law.

Identifying Learning-Disabled Students

The special education process in schools usually begins when teachers observe that students are struggling and falling behind their classmates. Yet even when they are on the verge of failure, identifying children with learning disabilities is rarely easy or straightforward. The federal government defines a "specific learning disability" as "a disorder in one or more of the basic psychological processes involved in understanding or in using language, spoken or written, that may manifest itself in an imperfect ability to listen, think, speak, read, write, spell, or to do mathematical calculations."[21] The phrase "imperfect ability" could apply to almost anyone who struggles in school. Teachers must use their professional judgment to filter out students who are having problems because of a learning disability from those with other issues. Language disabilities are most often identified in the second or third grades, at a time when children are expected to start reading and writing for meaning. When they are noticed at all, nonverbal and math-related disabilities tend to be identified around the same time, as children struggle to retain basic math facts.

Yet there are many students with learning disabilities who are never identified in the elementary years. Some children hide their disabilities from teachers and even family members out of shame or embarrassment. Some withdraw or sit quietly without disturbing the class, until they become frustrated and unhappy. Others, who are bright and capable, manage to get by with average work and are seen by teachers as lazy, when in fact they are underachieving because of a disability. In schools with a large number of low-income or minority students, or nonnative English speakers, children may be stereotyped as badly behaved or unmotivated. In contrast, in wealthier school districts, parents sometimes spend hours helping their children with homework, or hire private tutors to help them, which leaves teachers with the impression that they are doing fine.

Researchers warn that the failure to identify many learning-disabled students is extremely troubling, because early intervention can often save them from the shame and frustration

When a Teacher Makes a Difference

Patricia Polacco is an award-winning children's book illustrator and author who did not learn to read until she was almost fourteen years old. She hated school and was teased mercilessly. "I felt trapped in a body that wouldn't do what everybody else could do,"[1] she says. That was when one of her teachers came to the rescue. Polacco wrote a picture book titled *Thank You, Mr. Falker* as a tribute to that teacher. The book and illustrations tell the story of a girl named Trisha, who, just like Polacco, felt stupid in school. When Trisha moves to a new school during the fifth grade, she meets a teacher named Mr. Falker, who not only helps her understand her learning disability but also teaches her to be proud of her drawings. Mr. Falker would stand behind Trisha whenever she was drawing and whisper, "This is brilliant . . . absolutely brilliant. Do you know how talented you are?"[2] Mr. Falker also helps Trisha recognize her learning differences for the first time. "Don't you understand," he tells her, "[that] you don't see letters or numbers the way other people do[?]"[3] In the story, Mr. Falker enlists the support of a reading teacher, and together they work with Trisha every day at lunchtime until she learns to read.

1. Patricia Polacco. "Who Am I?" Patricia Polacco.com. www.patriciapolacco.com /author/bio/bio.html.
2. Polacco. "Who Am I?"
3. Patricia Polacco. *Thank You, Mr. Falker.* New York: Philomel, 1998, p. 19.

of academic failure. In recent years, federal laws have tried to address this concern by directing schools to adopt a new approach called "response to intervention" (RTI). With RTI, teachers screen all children in kindergarten and step in immediately to help those at risk for learning failure. The classroom teacher first tries different approaches to the material. If the student does not make progress, the teacher tries more-intensive, small-group instruction. At this point, a support teacher also works with the student individually. If the student still does not respond, he is then referred for testing and evaluation to determine whether he has a learning disability. Researchers are encouraged by RTI, but say it can only work on a large scale if classroom teachers across the country are trained to address many kinds of academic difficulties and to recognize when students are making progress and when they have a learning disability and need further support.

The Evaluation

When students fail to respond to early interventions, or when they are struggling and falling behind in class, teachers refer them for observation and testing to find out whether they are eligible for special education services. The formal evaluation is carried out by a team of school professionals, including a psychologist, a special educator, and, depending on the child's needs, a speech and language therapist or an occupational therapist or adaptive physical education teacher for concerns about fine and gross motor skills.

The first step in the evaluation is a meeting in which the team members, classroom teacher, and a school administrator talk to the child's parents or caregiver about their concerns. They also describe how the evaluation process will unfold, with observations of the student and a battery, or series, of tests. The parents or caregiver must agree to the evaluation and grant their permission in writing before the team members can observe the child in the classroom. If the child has social or behavioral issues, parents and teachers also fill out surveys rating his attitudes, attention span, moods, and social skills.

The next step is for the psychologist on the team to administer an aptitude or IQ test to measure the child's potential for learning. Most modern IQ tests are divided equally between verbal and nonverbal subtests, each of which carries equal weight toward the overall score. Among the verbal tasks, students might be asked to define vocabulary words, describe how words are alike or similar, and explain concepts or social situations that require practical judgment. On the nonverbal subtests, students might build 3-D structures with blocks, repeat sequences of numbers forwards and backwards, and respond to simple mental math problems.

The team calculates an overall IQ score that reflects how a child's performance on the test compares with those of peers of the same age and grade. For students with learning disabilities, this score is often misleading. The team discovers more about the child by looking at the scores on the different subtests. A student who struggles with visual tasks, for example, might score below average on the subtests that involve visual memory and perception and in the superior range on tasks involving vocabulary and verbal comprehension. His overall IQ is slightly above average, but this does not reflect his strong performance in reading and writing. In contrast, another student may score very high on nonverbal tasks, but struggle to decode words and read fluently. Her overall IQ falls in the average range, but the subtest results indicate a reading disability.

The Individualized Education Program (IEP) lists accommodations the child will receive, such as access to a computer to type or spell check work.

The scores on the IQ test are also compared with scores on an academic achievement test. The special educator on the team usually administers the achievement test, which covers the type of material students encounter in the regular classroom. They are asked to read words and passages out loud, calculate math problems, and answer factual questions in social studies, science, and other areas. The scores on this test can reveal how a learning disability is affecting performance in academic subjects.

The evaluators weigh many factors as they decide whether a child is eligible for special education services. They look for signs of underachievement, such as an unexpected gap between overall IQ and low achievement in one or more areas of the test. They consider whether the child is making sufficient progress in the subjects covered on the academic achievement test, and they relate all of this to his personal development, behavior, and performance in the classroom.

Sometimes teachers do not refer a child for evaluation, but rather the child's parents suspect that the child might have a learning disability. By law, they are entitled to request that the school carry out a formal evaluation. Parents who can afford it might also arrange for sessions with a private neuropsychologist, who conducts a similar but more comprehensive battery of tests and observations.

The Individualized Education Program

For learning-disabled students who qualify, schools are obligated by law to create an individualized education program, or IEP. The key word in an individualized education program is *individualized*. The IEP is like a road map that lays out annual academic and social goals for the individual student and the supports that will be put in place to help her achieve these goals. It can include any combination of special education and general education services that help the student gain access to the curriculum, including individual or small-group instruction once a week, several times a week, or daily in the school resource room. For example, Alison is a fourth grader with

Learning Disabilities on the Playground and Beyond

Some learning-disabled children excel outside of the classroom. They leave their reading or math difficulties behind when they kick a soccer ball or pirouette across a ballet studio. For other students, learning disabilities do not disappear when the school bell rings. They carry their disabilities with them on the playground or soccer field, when they rehearse for a school play, or practice the piano. In order to participate, they need extra support and accommodations. Like a good teacher, a supportive coach or instructor can often make a huge difference in building self-esteem and motivating learning-disabled students. Sometimes assistive technologies or other supports make a difference. There are book clubs that offer titles in audio formats so children with reading disabilities can take part. An online video that records the steps for a dance recital might help a learning-disabled student remember the choreography. In sports such as basketball or soccer a coach might ensure that a child understands the rules of the game by reviewing strategies or even running alongside the field and using hand signals until the child learns the rules. Taking part in these activities often helps learning-disabled children reach goals that they did not think they were capable of achieving.

In sports such as soccer a coach might ensure that a child understands the rules of the game by reviewing strategies, or even running alongside the field and using hand signals until the child learns the rules.

a language-based learning disability who also struggles with friendships. Her IEP states that she will attend sessions in the resource room for sixty minutes of reading and sixty minutes of speech and language work each week. She also meets with a guidance counselor once a week for a social-skills session, during which she is asked to role-play scenarios that she might encounter with peers in the classroom and on the playground.

One of the most important parts of the IEP document is a list of annual goals for the student. The goals in Alison's IEP focus on improving her reading and writing skills. These include that she will "decode single and multi-syllable words with 95 percent accuracy" and "will be able to state the main idea of what she has read in four out of five opportunities as observed by staff."[22] The IEP also lists any accommodations that the school will provide, including assistive technologies, such as a calculator or computer spelling dictionary. In Alison's case, these include extra time to finish a test and a seat in the front of the classroom to minimize distractions.

Learning to Read and Write

Most students with an IEP have a language-based learning disability, and one of the special education services they often need is extra reading support. In recent years, researchers have made dramatic progress in understanding what happens in the brain as people learn to read. They have discovered that the key to the entire reading process is a concept called "phonemic awareness," the understanding of how to manipulate the smallest units of sound, or phonemes, that are the building blocks of all spoken and written words. The word *bat*, for example, can be broken into the phonemes *b*, *aaa*, and *tuh*.

Researchers say that there are ways to assess whether students as young as preschool struggle with phonemic awareness and to begin to address the problem right away with intensive, small-group instruction. Many research-based reading programs are designed to help young children with reading disabilities, including some of the best known: Orton-Gillingham, Wilson, and Lindamood-Bell. In Orton-Gillingham, the lessons are highly structured and try to engage all of the senses as students learn about letters and sounds; for example, asking them to tap each finger to their thumbs as they sound out a word. In Lindamood-Bell, children learn about how the phonemes feel as they are physically formed with the lips, tongue, and palate. A *p* for example, is called a lip popper, because the lips start together and then move apart. Researchers say all of these programs can be effective if they offer consistent small-group or individual instruction; repeated exposure to phonemes, letters, and words; and plenty of reading practice to build fluency.

Children with math disabilities are helped if they are taught basic number sense in the early grades and learn to develop a number line in their heads.

Yet while reading programs like Orton-Gillingham have a proven track record, they are time and labor intensive and require teacher training. Most public schools are not able to offer this kind of instruction to all of the children who struggle to read. Sometimes parents hire tutors to work with students at home or pay to send their children to private schools, but the vast majority of students receive reading support in public schools, where the quality of instruction is unpredictable. The long-term Connecticut study on reading performance found that dyslexic students failed to show significant improvement in reading fluency even when they received years of special education services in school. The authors concluded that this was because the school services were inconsistent from year to year. "As common as reading problems are, and as much as we have learned about them," says the study's director, Sally Shaywitz, "dyslexia is often missed."[23]

When Students Struggle in Math

Research on math disabilities has not received nearly the level of attention as research on reading disabilities. Even when teachers observe that students in their classrooms are faltering in math, they may not be trained to address them in a way that makes a lasting difference for students.

In recent years, researchers have discovered a concept that they believe is as essential to success in math as phonemic awareness is to reading. This is the concept of "number sense," or the meaning and magnitude of numbers. Number sense is having a sense of what numbers mean and how large or small they are. It is also being able to represent the same number in many different ways and perform simple mental math without pencil or paper. Most children develop number sense informally, before they start kindergarten, through interactions with adults and other children. One child may start school knowing that seven is bigger than three, while a classmate may already have a strategy to figure out how much bigger, by counting on four fingers. Still other children, including many with learning disabilities, begin school with a very weak number sense and are unsure which number is bigger.

Yet researchers say that number sense, like phonemic awareness, can be taught to young children at risk for math disabilities. One method that has been successful is to help young children develop a number line in their heads so they can visualize addition and subtraction problems as they solve them. "The human mind has a limited capacity to process information," say researchers who believe all schools should offer number sense instruction. "If too much energy goes into figuring out what 9 plus 8 equals, little is left over to understand the concepts underlying multi-digit subtraction, long division, or complex multiplication."[24]

The Inclusion Classroom

In an inclusion classroom, even students with math and reading disabilities who need extra supports spend most or even all of their day with their nondisabled classmates. The general education teacher collaborates closely, and sometimes teaches side by side, with a special educator. Students take part in cooperative learning projects in which they work together and develop social relationships with everyone in the class, but they also often break into small groups for reading or math activities according to their ability levels. The idea is that struggling students get the help they need, while those who are more advanced can move ahead. Dr. Mara Sapon-Shevin, an educator and strong inclusion supporter, explains that this approach says to learning-disabled students, "You have a right to be here, this is your classroom and your school as much as any other student's. We will do what we need to make this classroom a safe, welcoming, and successful environment for you"[25]

While many teachers admire the values and goals of the inclusion classroom, the idea is controversial. For inclusion to work well, class size must be manageable, teachers must be trained to work with students of all ability levels, and school administrators must be fully behind the effort. But this is not the reality in many U.S. public schools. Special educators also say that full inclusion may not be suitable for students with

In an inclusion classroom the general education teacher collaborates closely, and sometimes teaches side by side, with a special educator, like the sign language interpreter in the picture.

severe learning issues or for those who have trouble getting along with their peers. Still, supporters insist that inclusion can work as long as schools allow teachers the time, creativity, and professional training to make instruction interesting and accessible for everyone in the classroom.

Good Teaching Makes a Difference

Even with inclusion classrooms and special methods of math and reading instruction, teachers are the ones who often have the greatest impact in motivating learning-disabled students. A caring, supportive teacher who affirms students' strengths and gives them a voice in the classroom can make the difference between success and failure in school.

The teachers who are most effective in supporting learning-disabled students often have the universal qualities of good teachers everywhere. They are compassionate and nonjudgmental but also have high expectations of their students. They help students discover their strengths instead of criticizing their weaknesses. When a dyslexic student submits an essay, they remark on the originality of the ideas rather than on the many spelling errors. They also intervene when students feel unimportant or silenced and bullied by peers. Even if children are uncomfortable raising their hands in class, these teachers find ways for them to express their opinions in journals, autobiographies, or through artwork or other media.

Liana, whose painful memories of growing up with a learning disability opened the first chapter of this book, is forever grateful to an English teacher who changed her outlook on school and life.

My sixth grade English teacher recognized that I could draw, creating worlds of my own where I could lose myself. She knew that I could also *write* about these things if given the chance. She taught me to love to write, even when no one, including me, could read my stories, because the spelling was so bad. I explained them to her, and she understood. Suddenly my best was good enough. I began to think maybe it was all right to try.[26]

A New Approach to Special Education

Skilled teachers will always have a positive influence on the lives of learning-disabled students, but some educators say that this is not enough. Schools must also do a better job of accommodating students who learn differently or do not conform to conventional ideas of intelligence, they say. Long ago, in the 1850s, a young boy named Thomas Edison grew frustrated with his one-room schoolhouse because it discouraged hands-on learning. "It was impossible to observe and learn the processes of nature by description, or the English alphabet and arithmetic only by rote," he wrote in his diaries. "It was always necessary to observe with my own eyes and do things or to make things."[27] While few students are likely to have the restless brilliance of a young Edison, educators have begun to

In the 1850s Thomas Edison (pictured) grew frustrated with his one-room schoolhouse because it discouraged hands-on learning by experience. Schools must do a better job of accommodating students who learn differently or do not conform to conventional ideas of intelligence, some educators say.

ask whether even today, in an era when students of diverse backgrounds and abilities often share a classroom, schools are flexible enough for children who have the potential to contribute to society in unexpected ways.

To address this concern, these educators advocate a new approach to special education in schools. Instead of treating children as if they are broken and in need of repair, they believe special education should concentrate on building children's strengths and teaching them strategies to cope with their difficulties. Education professor Thomas Hehir agrees. He interviewed learning-disabled students who were accepted into Harvard University to understand how they overcame their disabilities and succeeded in school. "They learned the same thing as everybody else in the class," he says about their grade school years, "but they were allowed to learn it in the ways that were most efficient for them."[28]

CHAPTER FIVE

Living and Coping with Learning Disabilities

"**I** don't know what it's like not to have dyslexia. I don't know that I want to do life over again without it. It's part of me. It will hinder me, as it has, and it will push me into places where I never would have gone."[29] For the thirty-three-year-old man who made this statement, dyslexia is as much a part of him as his personality or the color of his eyes.

The reality for learning-disabled children is that they will grow up to become learning-disabled adults. The difficulties they experience in childhood continue to affect them when they graduate from high school and move on to college or into the workplace. Achieving success in their personal and professional lives may depend on whether they can learn to accept that their disabilities are lifelong.

In recent years, many opportunities have opened up for adults with learning disabilities in areas of life that once would have been closed to them. More students with learning disabilities than ever before are graduating from high school and enrolling in two- or four-year public and private colleges and universities. As adults they are entering fields such as business, entertainment, medicine, education, the arts, media, science, and technology. They lead rewarding professional lives by accepting that their disabilities are part of who they are, but they do not allow themselves to become trapped or defined by them.

Adults with learning disabilities who achieve success in work and life tend to share certain characteristics and attitudes. A study at the Frostig Center, a California-based group dedicated to researching and helping people with learning disabilities, tracked forty learning-disabled students from childhood until twenty years after they graduated from high school. The authors discovered six "success attributes," including "self awareness, proactivity, perseverance, goal setting, using support systems, and emotional coping strategies"[30] that were more important than IQ scores or grades in predicting which of the students would lead productive, fulfilling lives as adults.

Other researchers agree that learning-disabled adults who achieve success in their personal and professional lives know how to ask for the supports and accommodations they need. They are independent but also recognize when they should seek the help and counsel of others. They have strong coping strategies to deal with frustration and failure, and a support network of family, friends, teachers, and colleagues to encourage them. Above all, they have a realistic understanding of their learning strengths and the challenges they face. "True acceptance of a learning disability," these researchers say, "includes the knowledge that life will be harder for the person living with it."[31]

Life After High School

In some special education programs, students have already begun to accept and understand the nature of their learning disabilities long before they graduate from high school. Once students turn sixteen, the school IEP must include a statement of how they will transition into adulthood. This statement reflects their own goals and visions for life as adults. Around this time, they are also encouraged to consider whether college is the right path for them. The majority of learning-disabled students move directly from high school into the workforce. Depending on their interests, a knowledgeable high school special education team can help direct them to vocational training or on-the-job apprenticeships.

While college is not a good fit for everyone with a learning disability, a growing number of learning-disabled students are finding that community colleges and universities are right for them. According to the U.S. Department of Education, as many as 9 percent of students attending U.S. colleges have some kind of learning disability, and the number is rising. Several small, private colleges consider it their mission to educate students with learning disabilities. Other colleges and universities have designated learning centers where disabled students receive academic tutoring, organizational help, and other supports. If students are on an IEP in high school, they may be entitled to accommodations on college entrance exams such as the SAT, including extra time to finish the test.

Often the biggest dilemma that learning-disabled students face during the college application process is whether or not

Many colleges and universities welcome learning-disabled students and offer them academic support in classrooms and learning centers.

to disclose that they have a disability. Some students decide to send a letter or write an essay explaining how they have managed to overcome a learning disability and excel in school and extracurricular activities. Yet most learning-disabled students elect not to disclose. Under the terms of the civil rights law, the Americans with Disabilities Act, it is illegal for colleges to ask about a disability. Learning-disabled students must be judged, just like all other applicants, on whether they meet the school's criteria for admissions.

Learning Disabilities in College

Once they are accepted, many learning-disabled students have a smooth transition to college life. They may have to study harder than others, but they also have a few advantages over their non-learning-disabled peers. Most have been evaluated in high school and have gained insights about how they learn best. They are also likely to have encountered situations in which they were forced to advocate for themselves, so they are less hesitant than other students to approach professors when they need help. Christopher Lee, author of the memoir *Faking It*, spent his school years trying to hide his disability from everyone before learning to advocate for himself in college. "I try to meet my teachers before the quarter begins. I let them know that what I tell them about my learning difficulties is confidential. I emphasize to them that I would rather not be singled out as a special student although I might need some class modifications. I mention a few of my weaknesses, but I emphasize my strengths,"[32] he writes.

For other learning-disabled students, the transition to college is a rocky one. They may feel overwhelmed trying to balance the academic demands of college life. If they struggle with social interactions, they may feel anxious about how they will get along with roommates or make new friends. Those who have always relied on parents to speak up and advocate for them may be unprepared to fight their own academic battles. Many are without the goals and supports of an IEP for the first time since early childhood.

Civil Rights for the Disabled: The Americans with Disabilities Act

"Let the shameful walls of exclusion finally come tumbling down," declared President George H.W. Bush as he signed the historic Americans with Disabilities Act (ADA) into law on July 26, 1990. The ADA is the world's first comprehensive declaration of civil rights for people with physical, mental, and learning disabilities. It was passed after decades of struggle on the part of injured war veterans, parents of children with disabilities, and Americans from all walks of life who joined a growing disability rights movement. They borrowed many of the same tactics used in the battle for civil rights in the 1960s, including peaceful sit-ins, marches, and lawsuits in state and federal courts that challenged the country's discriminatory laws and practices. The ADA bars discrimination against the disabled in employment, housing,

Yet while there are no IEPs in college, learning-disabled students are still protected by federal civil rights laws that make it illegal to discriminate against them or deprive them of equal access to an education. The protections of the Americans with Disabilities Act (ADA) are far-reaching and extend to disabled people of all ages in public and private schools and colleges, as well as in any workplace setting with more than fifteen employees. The difference is that the burden of proof shifts to the learning-disabled students themselves. This means that they are only protected if they disclose to college officials that they have a disability and provide evidence, such as a psychological evaluation, to back it up. Some students still choose not to disclose their disability in college, because they are eager to break free of the stigma of education, and transportation and forbids lack of access to public places such as restaurants, hotels, and hospitals. The results of the law are visible today in handicapped-accessible buses, ramps on buildings, and walk signals on traffic lights that beep for the visually impaired. They also include less visible but equally important changes such as the removal of barriers to employment and school admissions and the integration of people with physical, mental, and learning disabilities into all aspects of life.

George H.W. Bush. "Remarks of President George Bush at the Signing of the Americans with Disabilities Act," July 26, 1990. www.eeoc.gov/eeoc/history/35th/videos/ada_signing_text.html.

The Americans with Disabilities Act, signed into law in 1990, led to an increase in assistive devices such as the automatic door button (pictured).

having a disability, but this means they are no longer entitled to accommodations.

When students do disclose their disabilities, college officials are legally bound to provide reasonable accommodations. The term *reasonable* is not clearly defined in the ADA, which is why a student's self-awareness and self-advocacy skills are critical. Students are far more likely to succeed in college if they can explain their needs clearly and ask professors for accommodation, such as modifying testing formats or allowing them to record lectures or use assistive technologies in class.

Learning Disabilities in the Workplace

Self-awareness is also critical when people with learning disabilities search for a job. Those who have a clear sense of their strengths and weaknesses are more likely to set realistic career goals and find a job that is a good fit for their skills and abilities. A person with dyslexia but exceptional visual-spatial skills, for example, might decide to become an engineer or graphic designer. A person with a math disability but excellent verbal and writing skills might enter publishing or journalism.

Sometimes learning to accept a disability can mean rethinking a career goal that has been a lifelong dream. A college student long fascinated by marine science found herself failing biology classes because of a short-term memory deficit that interfered with the ability to recall scientific names and information. She abandoned the idea of becoming a scientist and instead realized that she had a natural gift for working with children. In other cases, learning-disabled students refuse to give up on a childhood dream. When a special educator tried to convince a college student with dyslexia that a career in veterinary medicine was a stretch for her, she only became more determined. "When I am going out of my mind trying to read a textbook or study for a test, I know the 'why' behind what I am doing," she says. "I know that in just a few years, I will be applying for med school and that every test I take, every book I read, every animal I heal, will be taking me toward my goal."[33]

Even in a job that is well suited to their needs, learning-disabled people often face challenges in the workplace. They may take longer than their colleagues to accomplish a task or grow overwhelmed trying to keep up with a heavy workload. If they have a language-learning disability, they may have trouble writing reports, taking messages, or reading instructions. They may also feel frustrated or worry about coworkers resenting them or making jokes at their expense.

Yet successful adults with learning disabilities also have traits that are highly valued in the workplace. They may have specialized talents such as drawing, mechanical skills, or public speaking. They also tend to be hardworking, resourceful, and creative problem solvers who think outside the box. They have developed these skills out of necessity over many years of finding ways to compensate for academic weaknesses.

Just as in a college situation, the hardest dilemma that many adults face in the workplace is whether to disclose to their employers that they have a disability. The ADA prohibits employers from discriminating against qualified individuals with disabilities in hiring, firing, promotion, salary, or other conditions of employment. (The only exception to this rule is if the disability would prevent someone from doing a job, even with accommodations.) Despite these protections, most adults do not risk disclosure during a job interview because it would be extremely difficult to prove that they were turned down because of discrimination. The employer can always argue that there was a better candidate for the job.

Instead, many adults choose to disclose that they have a disability and ask for accommodations only after they have been on the job for long enough to show that they are capable and motivated. The ADA mandates that employers, just like colleges, provide reasonable accommodations. These often include the same kind of supports that worked in the classroom, such as providing more structure, eliminating time limits, or moving a desk or office space away from distracting noises.

Getting Help from Assistive Technologies

Learning-disabled adults often meet the challenges of a job or college course with the help of assistive technologies. An assistive technology is any device used by people with learning or physical disabilities to perform tasks that might otherwise be difficult or impossible for them. Such technologies can range from low-tech equipment such as a calculator to more high-tech personal computing systems, voice recognition software, or global navigation and positioning systems (GPS). Assistive technologies open up jobs and educational opportunities for learning-disabled people where once few existed.

In an age in which new high-tech products constantly appear on the market, each promising something faster, more powerful, and more user-friendly, it is easy to fall under the spell of the latest device. Yet while technology greatly enhances learning, not every device is right for everyone with a disability.

Assistive technologies are most effective when they reinforce people's learning strengths, and diminish areas of weakness or challenge. For motor disabilities, these might include large pad keyboards or foot pedals that replace the mouse on a normal computer. For nonverbal disabilities, a GPS can be a lifesaver while driving or traveling. For dyslexia and other language-based learning disabilities, there are many technologies that remove barriers to reading and writing, including speech recognition software, spell-checkers, and outlining programs; screen readers that read articles from the Internet aloud; and scanners that capture text images such as a classroom hand-out, report, or even a restaurant menu.

Spurred on by his own struggles with dyslexia, businessman and designer Ben Foss helps create assistive technologies for people with language-learning disabilities. He also depends on assistive technology in his own work. "We need to use the tools and accommodations that are available to us to help us succeed," he says. To inspire others, Foss often shows people

Assistive technologies, like the global navigation and positioning system (GPS), can open up jobs and educational opportunities for learning-disabled people.

the raw version of his writing before technology helps him improve the text; for example, he writes: "It canbe scary to tell people that you are of part of a lable that is assocated with being lazy or stupid," he types without the benefit of a spell-checker, "I have fel this sting. . . . Eventually, you will be comfortable talking ro stragers about it. And then other people with LD [learning disabilities] will start coming to you, alloing you to be lart of something larger. It is a good feeling and is the most important accomidaiton you can have."[34]

Impact on Everyday Living

Even with assistive technologies for support, learning disabilities can interfere with everyday tasks that most people do not think twice about, like grocery shopping or leaving a tip at a restaurant. They can also make it difficult to carry out more important tasks, such as making financial decisions, keeping track of medications, driving, or forming trusting relationships. "My short-term memory problem means that I can't remember things like words, random numbers, people's names, grocery lists," says Sylvester. "I forget about chores that I'm supposed to do, and have trouble keeping track of time."[35]

The solutions to these problems may be as simple as always taking a list to the grocery store or posting a chart with medical information in the kitchen, or as complicated as learning how to interpret nonverbal facial expressions. Learning-disabled adults sometimes need to seek the support of social workers, job counselors, or psychologists to help them develop social skills or overcome their frustration and anxiety in the workplace.

For adults whose disabilities are severe, living independently can be a real challenge. If they have motor disabilities, they may not be able to drive and may have to rely on public transportation, such as buses and subways. If their disabilities are nonverbal, they may struggle to use money and credit cards properly. If they lack basic reading skills, they may be unable to read instructions, follow signs, or hold onto a steady job. Adults with severe learning disabilities often fall through the

Discovering a Learning Disability as an Adult

Many adults do not realize they have a learning disability until they are long past school age. Some grew up before the era of special education, while others were never identified in school because they hid their disabilities or managed to scrape by as underachievers. There are many reasons that adults may wonder whether they have a learning disability. They may meet someone with similar issues, hear about learning disabilities in the media, or find out that a child or other family member has a learning disability. Often being labeled as learning disabled brings a sense of relief: Finally, there is an explanation for why they performed poorly in school or on the job. Yet when they tell friends, family members, or employers about their disabilities, they often are met with resistance and disbelief.

Some may also need time and support to adjust to a new self-image. Painful memories of childhood or adolescence may resurface. It is not uncommon to feel anger or to blame parents for not recognizing the problem. It may be just as important to address the emotional health issues that arise when a learning disability is discovered late in life, as it is to ensure that the right educational or workplace accommodations are put in place.

cracks in the system. Without a support network, they may feel isolated and shunned by others.

In contrast, learning-disabled adults who achieve success in their lives have developed emotional coping strategies that they rely on when they are faced with the inevitable frustrations and disappointments of everyday life. The worst that people can do, says Oliver Queen, who has dyslexia, is let a learning disability become a scapegoat for everything that goes wrong: "Can't find a good job? Must be the LD. Relationships always fail? It's the LD. If you follow this destructive path," he warns, "you spend the remainder of your life being controlled by your LD."[36]

Family and Support Networks

Adults who refuse to let their disabilities dominate their lives often have a support network of family and friends who accept and encourage them along the way. These people are there to listen and offer support without reacting harshly or making judgments. At the same time, they steer the learning-disabled adults in their lives toward realistic goals and expectations.

It is often parents who have been there from the start who continue to root for their learning-disabled children, even as they become adults. They are the ones who navigate the pain of school failure and give children the academic and emotional support to thrive. In some cases, they may have experienced disappointment, denial, or, if they have a disability themselves, guilt when they first learned of their children's difficulties.

Yet many parents and family members learn to be flexible in their expectations and help ensure that their learning-disabled children lead successful lives as adults. For some learning-disabled people, their siblings, teachers, coaches, friends, and colleagues play a similar role in encouraging and supporting them. "It is from their encouragement that I found the strength to face my fears and become who I am," says Lynn Pelkey, a young woman with severe dyslexia. "While my disability will last my lifetime, it no longer has to limit me. I now strive to see myself as my parents see me."[37]

Learning-disabled adults who do not have parents, family members, or friends to advise and encourage them may turn to groups that offer support and advocate on their behalf. Many of these groups, including the Learning Disabilities Association of America and the National Center for Learning Disabilities, connect them with others who face similar challenges so they can exchange stories and experiences. They also provide legal advice in cases of workplace discrimination or direct people to vocational training and career-support services. While it is

Learning-disabled children are more likely to achieve success as adults if they have friends, family, teachers, and coaches to support and encourage them.

common to feel depressed or anxious because of a learning disability, the inspiring stories of others can often motivate people to seek the help and accommodations they need.

Toward a Greater Understanding

In spite of the many inspirational success stories of learning-disabled people, society has a long way to go before most learning-disabled people are understood and supported in school, work, and other aspects of life. As research contin-ues, some learning disabled hold out hope that scientists will discover more about the brain and devise medical treatments. Yet because every individual with a learning disability has a unique pattern of strengths and weaknesses, this is an unlikely scenario for the near future.

Instead of waiting for a cure, researchers who study and work with learning disabilities, say the focus should be on helping more learning-disabled people develop the attributes that are known to build success, including self-awareness, self-advocacy, and coping strategies to deal with frustration and failure. "LD is a label and, as a label, stereotypes will always surface," says Christie Jackson, a young woman who learned to accept her disability in college. "But that label is also part of me. It's as much a part of me as my middle name, as my smile, as my love of lilacs."[38]

Notes

Introduction: Learning Differently

1. Harry Sylvester. *The Legacy of the Blue Heron: Living with Learning Disabilities.* Farmington, ME: Oxton House, 2002, p. 8.

Chapter One: What Is a Learning Disability?

2. Liana Mulholland. "A Hunger for Reading." National Center for Learning Disabilities. Success Stories, September 10, 2009. www.ncld.org/es/ld-basics/success-stories/anne -ford-allegra-ford-scholars/hunger-for-reading.
3. Larry B. Silver. "What Are Learning Disabilities?" Reading Rockets, 2001. www.readingrockets.org/article/5821.
4. Nelson Lauver. *Most Unlikely to Succeed: The Trials, Travels and Ultimate Triumphs of a "Throwaway" Kid.* New York: Five City Media, 2011, p. 9.
5. Edward M. Hallowell. Foreword to *Learning Outside the Lines* by Jonathan Mooney and David Cole. New York: Simon & Schuster, 2000, p. 17.

Chapter Two: Types of Learning Disabilities

6. Harold McGrady, Janet Lerner, and Mary Lynn Boscardin. "The Educational Lives of Students with Learning Disabilities." In *Learning Disabilities & Life Stories.* Pano Rodis, Andrew Garrod, and Mary Lynn Boscardin, eds. Boston: Allyn and Bacon, 2001, p. 178.
7. Christopher Lee and Rosemary Jackson. *Faking It: A Look into the Mind of a Creative Learner.* Portsmouth, NH: Boynton/Cook, 1992, p. 11.
8. Lee and Jackson. *Faking It*, p. 21.
9. Samantha Abeel. *My Thirteenth Winter: A Memoir.* New York: Scholastic, 2004, p. 22.

10. Tera Kirk. Tera's NLD Jumpstation. www.reocities.com
    /HotSprings/Spa/7262.
11. Lauver. *Most Unlikely to Succeed*, p. 69.
12. Lauver. *Most Unlikely to Succeed*, p. 250.

Chapter Three: The History of Learning Disabilities

13. Sylvester. *Legacy of the Blue Heron*, pp. 21–22.
14. Grace Fernald. *Remedial Techniques in Basic School
    Subjects*. New York: McGraw-Hill, 1943, p. 5.
15. Samuel A. Kirk. "Behavioral Diagnosis and Remediation
    of Learning Disabilities." In *Proceedings of the Confer-
    ence on Exploration into Problems of the Perceptually
    Handicapped Child*, Chicago, 1963.
16. Author interview with Barbara Lieber, October 15, 2011.
17. L.M. Dunn. "Special Education for the Mildly Retarded—
    Is Much of it Justifiable?" *Exceptional Children*, vol. 35,
    1968, pp. 5–22.
18. An Act to Amend the Education of the Handicapped Act
    to Provide Educational Assistance to all Handicapped
    Children, and for Other Purposes, Public Law 94-142. 94th
    Congress, November 29, 1975. Section 612. www.eric.ed
    .gov/PDFS/ED116425.pdf.
19. Lynn Pelkey. "In the LD Bubble." In *Learning Disabili-
    ties & Life Stories*. Pano Rodis, Andrew Garrod, and
    Mary Lynn Boscardin, eds. Boston: Allyn and Bacon,
    2001, p. 21.

Chapter Four: Learning Disabilities in School

20. Gerald R. Ford. "Statement on Signing the Education
    for All Handicapped Children Act of 1975," December 2,
    1975. Ford Library and Museum. www.ford.utexas.edu
    /library/speeches/750707.htm.
21. The Individuals with Disabilities Education Act. Public
    Law 108-446-118 Statute 2658, December 3, 2004. Section
    602, Definitions. http://nichcy.org/wp-content/uploads
    /docs/PL108-446.pdf.

22. IEP document for fourth-grade student in Lexington, Massachusetts, 2005.
23. Sally Shaywitz. *Overcoming Dyslexia: A New and Complete Science-Based Program for Reading Problems at Any Level.* New York: Knopf, 2003, p. 131.
24. Russell Gersten and David J. Chard. "Number Sense: Rethinking Arithmetic Instruction for Students with Mathematical Disabilities." Reading Rockets. www.reading rockets.org/article/5838.
25. Quoted in *Education World.* "Making Inclusion the Norm." Wire Side Chat. www.educationworld.com/a_issues/chat /chat206.shtml.
26. Mulholland. "A Hunger for Reading."
27. Quoted in Larry B. Silver. *The Misunderstood Child: Understanding and Coping with Your Child's Learning Disabilities.* New York: Three Rivers, 2006, p. 404.
28. Quoted in Jon Marcus. "The Test Ahead." *Boston Globe Magazine,* Education Issue October 9, 2011, p. 26.

Chapter Five: Living and Coping with Learning Disabilities

29. Quoted in Marshall H. Raskind and Roberta J. Goldberg. "Life Success for Students with Learning Disabilities: A Parent's Guide." LDOnline, 2005, p. 4. www.ldonline.org /article/12836.
30. Raskind and Goldberg. "Life Success for Students with Learning Disabilities."
31. McGrady, Lerner, and Boscardin. "The Educational Lives of Students with Learning Disabilities," p. 185.
32. Lee and Jackson, *Faking It,* p. 19.
33. Mackenzie Meyer. "The Gift of Learning Differently." National Center for Learning Disabilities Online. Success Stories, April 28, 2010. www.ncld.org/ld-basics/success -stories/anne-ford-allegra-ford-scholars/the-gift-of-learning -differently.
34. Quoted in NCLD Editorial Staff. "Interview with Ben Foss: How Self-Advocacy Can Lead to Innovation." National Center for Learning Disabilities, September 27, 2010. www.ncld.org/ld-basics/success-stories/adults-with

-ld/interview-with-ben-foss-how-self-advocacy-can-lead-to
-innovation.

35. Sylvester, *Legacy of the Blue Heron*, p. 46.
36. Oliver Queen. "Blake Academy and the Green Arrow." In *Learning Disabilities & Life Stories*. Pano Rodis, Andrew Garrod, and Mary Lynn Boscardin, eds. Boston: Allyn and Bacon, 2001, p. 15.
37. Lynn Pelkey. "In the LD Bubble," p. 28.
38. Christie Jackson. "Look in the Mirror and See What I See." In *Learning Disabilities & Life Stories*. Pano Rodis, Andrew Garrod, and Mary Lynn Boscardin, eds. Boston: Allyn and Bacon, 2001, p. 49.

Glossary

assistive technology: Any technology used by people with learning or physical disabilities in order to perform tasks that might otherwise be difficult or impossible for them.

central cortex (also called cerebral cortex): The part of the brain that directs the thinking and emotional functions. It is divided into halves called hemispheres that oversee all forms of conscious experience, including perception, language, motor skills, thinking skills, and organization skills.

cognition: Thinking, or the mental processes by which knowledge and understanding are gained through reasoning, experience, and sense perception.

executive function: The set of mental processes that people use to regulate behaviors and accomplish tasks. Executive function is involved in planning, monitoring, organizing, evaluating, and adjusting course as needed to get a job done.

inclusion: An approach to educating students with learning and other disabilities in which students spend most or all of their time in a regular classroom with their nondisabled peers, and a special educator collaborates with the classroom teacher in the disabled students' instruction. Inclusion is based on the right of all children to participate fully in the classroom and to have access to the full curriculum.

individualized education plan (IEP): An IEP is a legally binding document that schools must create for students who qualify for special education. It is designed to meet the child's unique learning and social needs and describes goals, supports, and accommodations the child will receive to help him/her access the curriculum.

mainstreaming: The practice of educating students with disabilities in regular classrooms. In contrast to the inclusion model, there is little effort made to modify the curriculum or provide classroom supports to help learning-disabled students gain better access to learning.

multisensory instruction: Instruction that engages all of the pathways of perception, including visual, auditory, and kinesthetic (movement), to reinforce learning and short-term memory.

neurology: The medical science that involves study of the nervous system and treatment of nervous system disorders.

neuron: A nerve cell.

phonemic awareness: The understanding of how to use and manipulate the smallest units of sound, or phonemes, which are the building blocks of all spoken and written words.

psychologist: A professional who studies human behavior and provides therapy and support for people with mental health and emotional issues. A school psychologist is involved in testing and evaluating students for learning disabilities.

special education: Instruction designed to meet the unique needs of students with learning and other disabilities. It involves individually planned and small group instruction and monitoring of students' progress. Sometimes, special education takes place in the regular classroom, but often it is handled in a school resource room.

special educator: A teacher, such as a reading or math specialist, who has been trained to work with students with learning and other disabilities.

Organizations to Contact

Children and Adults with ADD (CHADD)

8181 Professional Pl., Ste. 201
Landover, MD 20785
Phone: (301) 306-7070; toll-free: (800) 233-4050
Fax: (301) 306-7090
Website: www.chadd.org

CHADD is the country's largest nonprofit group serving children and adults with ADD/ADHD by providing them with resources, support, and advocacy.

Dyspraxia Foundation USA

3059 N. Lincoln Ave., Unit C
Chicago, IL 60657
Phone: (312) 489-8628
Website: www.dyspraxiausa.org

The group's website provides information and personal stories for individuals and families living with the fine and gross motor disabilities known as dyspraxia.

The Frostig Center

971 N. Altadena Dr.
Pasadena, CA 91107
Phone: (626) 791-1255
Fax: (626) 798-1801
Website: www.frostig.org

A nonprofit organization that specializes in working with children who have learning disabilities through its school and programs in California, this group also conducts research on the causes and effects of learning disabilities.

Headstrong Nation

E-mail: ben.foss@headstrongnation.org
Website: www.headstrongnation.org

Founded by assistive technology pioneer Ben Foss, Headstrong Nation is an online community for individuals with dyslexia. The site provides information about dyslexia in accessible multimedia formats, teaches self-advocacy skills, and promotes assistive technologies.

International Dyslexia Association (IDA)

40 York Rd., 4th Fl.
Baltimore, MD 21204
Phone: (410) 296-0232
Fax: (410) 321-5069
Website: www.interdys.org

IDA is a nonprofit group dedicated to helping people with dyslexia, their families, and the communities that support them.

Learning Disabilities Association of America (LDA)

4156 Library Rd.
Pittsburgh, PA 15234
Phone: (412) 341-1515
Fax: (412) 344-0224
Website: www.ldanatl.org

LDA is the largest nonprofit volunteer organization that advocates for people with learning disabilities, with over two hundred state and local chapters nationwide.

Project Eye-to-Eye

250 W. Ninety-Third St., Suite 17B
New York, NY 10025
Phone: (212) 537-4429
Fax: (480) 393-5416
Website: www.projecteyetoeye.org

A national nonprofit mentoring group that connects learning-disabled college students and recent graduates with learning-disabled children across the country to build self-esteem and self-advocacy skills.

U.S. Department of Education Office of Special Education and Rehabilitative Services (OSERS)

400 Maryland Ave. SW
Washington, DC 20202-7100
Phone: (202) 245-7468
Website: www2.ed.gov/about/offices/list/osers/osep/index.html

This federal agency is the division of the U.S. Department of Education that provides research and support to parents, individuals, school districts, and states in the areas of special education and vocational services.

For More Information

Books

Samantha Abeel. *My Thirteenth Winter: A Memoir.* New York: Scholastic, 2003. Written for young adult readers, this is a compelling account of one girl's struggles with dyscalculia and nonverbal learning disability. Abeel could not tell time, count out change, or remember a phone number in middle school, yet she had a gift for language and learned to express herself in poetry and writing.

Barbara P. Guyer. *The Pretenders: Gifted People Who Have Difficulty Learning.* Homewood, IL: High Tide, 1997. Guyer is a special educator who relates, with compassion and warmth, the inspiring personal stories of eight people who came to her to learn to read and write after they first struggled for years to hide their learning disabilities, even from friends and family.

Nelson Lauver. *Most Unlikely to Succeed: The Trials, Travels, and Ultimate Triumphs of a "Throwaway" Kid.* New York: Five City Media, 2011. Lauver is a radio broadcaster, humorist, and motivational speaker. In this memoir, he tells a heartbreaking story of growing up as a dyslexic child in a small town in Pennsylvania in the 1960s and being bullied, severely beaten, and ridiculed by teachers and students at school.

Sandra Augustyn Lawton, ed. *Learning Disabilities Information for Teens.* Detroit: Omnigraphics, 2006. Part of a series on teen health, this book is a compilation of excerpts from publications on learning disabilities issued by government and nonprofit groups such as the Learning Disabilities Association of America. It offers information and advice on the common signs and causes of learning disabilities, how to handle school and workplace issues, and organizations to contact for support.

Christopher Lee and Rosemary Jackson. *Faking It: A Look into the Mind of a Creative Learner.* Portsmouth, NH: Boynton/Cook, 1992. This inspiring memoir relates how Lee faked his way through his school years with severe dyslexia and eventually came to accept his learning differences in college with the support of Jackson, a special educator, who also taught him to value his strengths.

Penny Hutchins Paquette and Cheryl Gerson Tuttle. *Learning Disabilities: The Ultimate Teen Guide.* Lanham, MD: Scarecrow, 2003. Part of a series called It Happened to Me, this book addresses teens directly and answers general questions about learning disabilities. Intended as a resource book, it includes an overview and history section, tips for success, inspiring quotes, first-person stories, and organizations to contact.

Patricia Polacco. *Thank You, Mr. Falker.* New York: Philomel, 1998. A picture book written for older elementary students, but inspiring for teens as well, in which well-known children's author and illustrator Polacco tells a story, based on her own life, of a girl with dyslexia who hides her disability until a compassionate fifth grade teacher recognizes her talent for drawing and helps her learn to read.

Harry Sylvester. *Legacy of the Blue Heron: Living with Learning Disabilities.* Farmington, ME: Oxton House, 2002. This book by a former president of the Learning Disabilities Association of America is divided into two sections. The first is the author's moving personal account of growing up with severe dyslexia in rural Maine in the 1930s and 1940s. The second offers his solutions for the problems faced by learning-disabled people today.

Websites

Kidshealth (www.kidshealth.org/teen/diseases_conditions /learning/learning_disabilities.html). A popular website for information about the health, behavior, and development of children and teens. The site includes articles in either audio or text format on topics related to learning disabilities, such as dyslexia, test anxiety, attention deficit/hyperactivity disorder (ADHD), and going to college.

LDonline (www.ldonline.org). An educational service of the public television station WETA-TV in Washington, D.C., in association with the National Joint Committee on Learning Disabilities, LDonline is a leading resource for information on learning disabilities and ADHD. The site includes up-to-date articles, first-person essays by teens and adults, children's artwork, question-and-answer forums, and links to other websites and organizations.

National Center for Learning Disabilities (www.ncld.org). A website with information and resources for individuals with learning disabilities, their parents, and teachers, this site includes articles, glossaries, recent research, audio stories and podcasts, first-person essays, and student artwork.

National Dissemination Center for Children with Disabilities (www.nichcy.org). This website provides information about children and youth with disabilities, including fact sheets, resources, and discussion of laws such as the Individuals with Disabilities Education Act (IDEA).

U.S. Department of Education, Office of Special Education Program's IDEA Website (idea.ed.gov/explore /home). This site was created to provide resources and information related to the Individuals with Disabilities Education Act (IDEA), including searchable versions of IDEA and a question-and-answer forum.

Wrightslaw (www.wrightslaw.com) A website created by two law professors who specialize in special education law and advocacy, it includes articles and resources for parents, teachers, and professionals who work with learning-disabled students. It also links to a state-by-state directory that lists service providers, tutors, and other resources for learning-disabled kids.

Index

Picture Credits

About the Author

Meryl Loonin has written books for children and teens, including three previous titles for Lucent: *Hot Topics: Overweight America*, *Multicultural America*, and *Legalizing Drugs*. She has a background in documentary film and TV production and a master's degree in education. She has also collaborated on websites and other creative work by and for kids. Loonin lives with her husband, Neil; two teenage children, Hana and Jonah; and a dog, Lexie, named for her hometown of Lexington, Massachusetts.